PRAISE FOR
NAVIGATING YOUR NEXT CAREER MOVE

"I was fortunate to work with Sonja when my team was struggling during some difficult growing pains. Our work with Sonja enabled me to be a more effective leader, and her insight and candor helped my staff and me move forward together. I cannot recommend her enough—her approach to leadership, rooted in honesty and trust, has helped our team continue to thrive and grow, even during the pandemic."

—Sally M. Joyner
Legal Director, Mid-South Immigration Advocates

"*Navigating Your Next Career Move* echoes the executive coaching Sonja provides by encouraging me to identify, reflect on, and find ways to shift my approaches to enhance my leadership skills, enabling me to inspire and motivate my team through strategic vision and shared goals for the future."

—Marcia LoMonaco
Head of People, FSG

"Sonja Mustiful offers us essential strategies for business leaders and executives looking to advance to the next level. Through her work, I appreciate how she cultivates audiences and gives them indispensable confidence to become effective leaders in their careers today and in the future."

—Marja Martin-Carruth
MEd, Director, Fogelman College of Business &
Economics at University of Memphis

"Sonja Mustiful shares how she simultaneously challenges, supports, and inspires those around her to succeed. She personally helped me to recognize and address my blind spots to become a transformational leader. *Navigating Your Next Career Move* is a true reflection of how Sonja excels at helping to fashion workable plans to achieve career goals."

—David Aubrey
VP of Finance, Elbit of America

Navigating Your Next Career Move

NAVIGATING YOUR NEXT CAREER MOVE

TAKING IT TO THE NEXT LEVEL

Sonja D. Mustiful

BOOKLOGIX·
Alpharetta, GA

ISBN: 978-1-6653-0462-7

⊗This paper meets the requirements of ANSI/NISO Z39.48-1992 (Permanence of Paper)

093022

This one is for my leadership squad.

Hold the vision, trust the process.
—Unknown

CONTENTS

FOREWORD

Career advice to my younger self: You are in for a roller coaster ride so buckle up. The career path you think you want now will change. Don't fight it; the change is good. Be prepared for some hard lessons. Each will make you stronger. Always, and I mean ALWAYS, stand up for yourself. Mistakes will happen along the way, and although you will think life as you know it is over, you will survive. Take the leaps, push for change (but not on your first day), and never stop reaching back and rising to your potential.

To my future self: Timing is everything. Stay the course, do what brings you joy, and don't let anything break your soul!

INTRODUCTION

What a difference two years have made! So much joy and gratitude have happened since the release of my first book, *Aim High, Ask Why: Discover Strengths, Uncover Blind Spots, Rise to Your Potential*. I had no idea how much publicity went into the release of a new book. After my first book's release date in 2019, I was whisked away on a media whirlwind, sharing insights about my new book. The whirlwind included a book cover design celebration dinner, my first television broadcast, a radio show interview, and, lastly, a book release interview with a local news anchor, just to name a few.

These media experiences were a true testament to how life has a way of showing up for you. I am so grateful for the many people who promoted the book, started book clubs, and were cheering me on for this next book release.

Whether you embark on a new year, consider another career path, or experience life-changing events, there will come a time to take your leadership to the next level. I wrote this book to share insights on how best to navigate your next career move in a world of ambiguity. Who knew we would have to pivot during a pandemic? The world experienced many epidemics in 2020 and 2021, from COVID-19 to racial instability to climate change. The constant in all this change is that there will continue to be various levels of change. How will you show up for yourself and the world around you? Learning does not stop because of a pandemic. That is in fact where the true development begins. Whether you work from home or are now homeschooling or changing careers, continue to focus on your career development and leaving a legacy.

The essence of why I wanted to write *Navigating Your Next*

Career Move was centered around holding space and providing a platform for leaders seeking ways to take their leadership to the next level. That level includes having intentional conversations that inspire individuals and teams to rise to their potential. Leading through a pandemic, and the impact of the Great Reshuffle, leaders are faced with the changing role of workplaces as organizations continue to redesign work. This is a huge transformation, reimagining a work design that encourages sustainable high-performance is essential to building the workforce of the future. *Navigating Your Next Career Move* provides insight on how *you*, the leader, can build greater resilience, level up your skill set, and incorporate professional development into your lifestyle. Take your career to the next level by expanding your career network, modeling transparency and authenticity, and celebrating your successes along the way.

Leadership gaps continue to widen, and it is so important that you are intentional about developing your skills to align with the skills needed for the future. Having the ability to lead through uncertainty is pivotal to personal adaptability and navigating complexity. Are you an innovative leader? Reskilling is your opportunity for fostering innovation and leveraging digitization.

A key learning I shared in my first book, *Aim High, Ask Why*, is that as you progress in your career, there are some things that you may want to unlearn. Unlearn some mindsets and skill sets to expand your thinking from a fixed mindset to a growth mindset. I included a note to leaders at the end of each chapter for leaders to put their leadership into action. Mindset determines your motivation and your elevation.

My company, Essence of Coaching, continues to embed leadership solutions that shift mindsets, behaviors, and practices toward inclusive leadership for individuals, teams, and organizations. Leaders need tools, resources, and support as they expand their ability to manage conflict, build empathetic relationships, and embrace differences.

As you read this book, spend time thinking about what makes

you genuinely happy in your career. What has been your biggest life lesson? How did you learn it? What is your purpose?

Reflect on ways to challenge your blind spots, remain curious about your current thinking, and understand what may be holding you back so you can create a path forward.

My hope is that you will reread the chapters of this book, reference it often in your career planning sessions, and recommend it as a must-read to business professionals who seek guidance on how to take charge of their careers and rise to their potential.

My intention is that, through my career love language of books, I have opened space for you to be inspired, motivated, and empowered as I speak my truths on taking your career to the next level.

"Our visions begin with our desires."
— Audre Lorde

CHAPTER ONE

LEADERSHIP VISION

What is a leader? A leader can be defined as "a powerful person who controls or influences what other people do; a person who leads a group or organization."[1] The leader of the future, in my opinion, is a person who sees the best in others, expects the best of themselves, and strives to empower the team toward greatness. Transformational leadership inspires a team toward a shared vision of the future. Transformational leaders are highly visible, and they spend a lot of time communicating. They don't necessarily lead from the front, as they tend to delegate responsibility among their team. And while their enthusiasm is often infectious, they will often need to be supported by people who love the details.

Transformational leaders have a clear set of admirable values and live those values in everything they do. This ability builds trust between them and team members. Transformational leaders know how to motivate people in a powerful fashion. They do this in four main ways:

---

[1] Definitions of leadership. (n.d.). Retrieved June 15, 2022, from https://www.tlu.ee/~sirvir/IKM/The%20Concept%20of%20Leadership/definitions_of_leadership.html.

- They have high standards and challenge team members to meet or exceed those standards. This provides a strong and uniting sense of purpose. Such leaders are unfailingly and realistically optimistic. To their core, they know goals can be met and obstacles can be overcome.
- Transformational leaders communicate clearly on every level. They have the ability to paint a compelling picture of the future in such a way that team members know exactly what the goals are, and what their roles are in achieving those goals.
- Transformational leaders have a "big picture" view and do everything within their power to connect team members, the organization, and themselves to that view.
- Transformational leaders have the ability to truly listen to the needs and concerns of individual members of the team.

WHAT'S YOUR LEADERSHIP VISION?

As I shared in my first book, *Aim High, Ask Why*, this book will also be filled with thought-prompting questions like: What's your vision? Where do you see your career or business in the next five to ten years? How will you know what is the best path forward? In *Navigating Your Next Career Move*, I will continue to ask questions that allow you time to reflect on how best to apply the learnings in real-time.

What if you are uncertain about your next career move? Consider the life around you. If you are at a turning point in your career, a point where you are expecting significant changes to occur, take this opportunity to reboot and reflect. Notice what keeps showing up around you that aligns with your vision. I can assure you, these are not coincidences; they are confirmations.

If you have a team you manage, do each of your team members know and understand your vision? For entrepreneurs, your business may have been hit first and worst or last and least with the economic downturn. How do you rebound? Think about how your vision aligns with today's business digitalization.

Carl Jung wrote, "Your vision will become clear only when you can look into your own heart. Who looks outside, dreams, who looks inside, awakens."[2]

In *Navigating Your Next Career Move*, as mentioned in my first book, *Aim High, Ask Why*, I share real-life stories and proven strategies from my fifteen-plus years as an HR corporate executive on how to reinvent yourself and remain relevant in your career.

In writing *Navigating Your Next Career Move*, I had the opportunity to share additional career experiences from colleagues, internal and external, to the field of human resources. What I found is that through our shared experiences, we have similar career-defining moments. We all have faced disappointment. How do you get back up? We all have experienced the juggling of competing priorities. How do you decide which task to start with? The universal takeaway from all of these conversations is that the right things happened in your career at the right time for the right reasons.

The Leadership Vision for many months in 2021 was centered around a Zoom meeting lens. Every organization had to quickly reassemble and develop technical tools that were conducive to multiple learning and meeting styles.

The new year may have started with one company vision, but

---

[2] Purrington, A. M., Published by Mr. Purrington Lifelong interest in Depth Psychology and the work of Carl Jung View all posts by Mr. Purrington, Purrington, P. by M., Purrington, M., Lifelong interest in Depth Psychology and the work of Carl Jung View all posts by Mr. Purrington, & View all posts by Mr. Purrington. (2021, June 15). *Carl Jung: "Who looks outside dreams; who looks inside awakes."* Carl Jung Depth Psychology. Retrieved June 15, 2022, from https://carljungdepthpsychologysite.blog/2020/02/08/carl-jung-i-am-afraid-that-the-mere-fact-of-my-presence-takes-you-away-from-yourself/.

then it quickly shifted to how best to survive in the world of virtual conference call mania. While there were many technical platforms used for conducting virtual team meetings, Zoom continued to be the meeting platform of choice.

What you focus on expands. It can be easy when you're in the midst of a challenge to just focus on the obstacles that are in front of you. But it's important not to get stuck staring at your obstacles or you'll end up stumbling over them. Instead, look past the obstacles and remember your vision. An authentic vision energizes you and pulls you forward. So, when you make your vision the focus instead of your obstacles, it puts things in proper perspective.

Do I actually want to return to the normal that I had, or am I noticing something in the midst of this new normal that I would actually like to keep?

As I have thought about this question over the last year, my perspective has shifted from some ambiguity to there are now so many unknowns. Having life stop unexpectedly leaves you with questions about what is really important for me and my career. I find myself more informed and engaged because now the "busyness" has been removed and "stay in place" has taken center stage.

When I reflected on my coaching business, I could see work from a different perspective because I have identified alternate ways to serve others from virtual workspaces. This included my one-on-one coaching sessions and leadership development workshops. A slower, simpler lifestyle has its advantages, like more creativity and less time in traffic. When the opportunity for a different lifestyle seems to be drawing near, I'm not so sure I'll be in a rush to get back to the way things were. I'd like to create a new and improved version of "normal" from the lessons learned during this time.

How about you? I challenge you to take some time to reflect and ask yourself, "How will you make your career more of what you want it to be?" When you take the time to focus and make improvements in your career, you open up opportunities for your career to expand.

Explore more. Grab your thought pad. Write down what you have envisioned for your career right now. Now that you have written that down, grab another sheet of paper. I want you to write down a vision that you have not thought of until just now. Write down something big. Think outside your realm of possibility. Do not worry about who may be watching. This is your vision; you have a blank canvas. Do not limit yourself to one sheet of paper or even one idea. Keep a notebook by your nightstand, if needed, to capture late night or early morning thoughts.

Now, what will it take for you to take the first step and put your idea(s) into action? You will not need a fancy GPS device. However, it will be helpful for leaders to design their new "internal" GPS embedded with both IQ and EQ to be more resilient and self-aware.

You do not have to follow an exploration manual. If there was a manual or direct path to our careers, we would have arrived at our destinations by now. Remember to "aim high, ask why," and it will all be worth seeing what the end will be.

What are some of the challenges that hold business professionals back, reassess their vision or cause them to seek other career opportunities? Emotional exhaustion, an overwhelming number of responsibilities, and declining employee morale are some of the challenges that leaders are faced with on a daily basis.

What are the things that you will carry forward with you from year to year and not go back to the way things used to be? What are you learning about yourself? What are you learning about your family and others close to you? What wisdom do you take from year to year that you don't want to forget?

After you've given yourself time to reflect, and once things really do begin to go back to some aspect of a "routine," you can begin to blend the pieces of your old habits that you've been excited about with the pieces of a new normal that have been refreshing to you. The old normal was not necessarily all good, and the new normal isn't necessarily all bad, so what will you take with you from year to year? Important questions to consider as you move forward on your vision statement.

As I mentioned at the beginning of this chapter, what you focus on expands. Make sure you are putting energy into that which will propel you forward.

You have the vision; now just imagine how you turn that dream into a reality. Expand your imagination to design realistic outcomes. You can test those outcomes with your leadership squad (discussed in Chapter 2). Conversely, have you prepared yourself for your next move? For instance, your dream job may not lead you to a promotion or a director-level position. First, it may be necessary to make sure you are positioned to receive the next opportunity by taking professional development classes, building essential networks, and working on your certification or advanced degree. How do you make your dream a reality? Let's say for instance you want to work for one of the top "one hundred best places to work" in your local area. You researched the company, prepared for the interview, and got your foot in the door.

The flip side of that reality is once you got your "foot in the door," you realized that you now have more doors to open. Growth and comfort do not coexist. As you move about on the path to reach your goal, you will have discomfort. Keep your motivational audiobooks set on speed dial in your car.

The truth is that no matter how hard you plan or what steps you take to "see it before you see it," your career vision mantra, you may run into roadblocks. Those twists and turns only make you stronger and wiser. Be prepared for your next step or decide on how to execute your Plan B and then respond accordingly.

Take time to explore what you want to do instead of what you want to be. Working diligently toward something you love is called passion. Do what you love. Love what you do.

What is the kind of work that motivates you? Are there problems you want to solve or challenges you want to overcome? If you start from a place of curiosity and ask yourself, "What if you had the opportunity to create your ideal position?" I had to start by being honest with myself. I wanted a career change but making a decision like that felt so overwhelming and scary that it seemed easier to just ignore my desires and pretend that the life I was living was indeed the life I wanted. Get honest in your answers about what you want, what you're afraid of, and what you might be avoiding. When you focus on what you really want, you can begin the process of a more authentic and powerful life.

You may find out that there may be multiple paths or destinations to reach your goal. The path to your success usually encompasses a partnership between you and your company/manager. Ultimately, you must take responsibility for and own your career development. The career development process involves ongoing planning, monitoring of key milestones, and making course corrections based on your personal ambitions and goals. You can start today and work toward refining the skills to get you focused on what you want to do. Begin by using new leadership development tools and sharpen the old ones to build new pathways to your next career level.

All of us have had encounters that caused us to pause or second guess our abilities. Why didn't I get that promotion? How come I was not asked to lead the project? Do you have a career strategy? Throughout this book, I will share previous and recent strategies that helped drive the trajectory of my career forward.

As I expanded my team, I not only communicated my vision with each team member, but I also shared my vision of their success within the company. Your team members need to know what is in it for them and the importance of their role in the company.

Think about a vision that has inspired you. Now think about what made it memorable and motivating. A sense of belonging to a team that clearly articulates the vision and sets out to move the goals forward is very impactful. Encourage the team to do a system goal check. Does our vision align with the future needs of our clients? It is always the right time to do your due diligence on your career.

The year 2020 was a journey of highs and lows. At the beginning of March 2020, I went on a social media hiatus. I needed space from all the negative headlines. Each negative narrative was causing a red alert for me. While the earth was moving at its normal pace, I found myself not wanting to keep up and needed to retreat to silence. I did not have any insight on the number of pandemics or epidemics the world would face, nor what my response needed to be.

During the downtime of 2020 when we were asked to stay in place, after much reflection, I was able to reassess my vision. During this time and space, I was fortunate to listen, feel, and learn from my inner voice on how best to move forward. You know, that voice that tells you to go this way, or that way, slow down, or do all three at the same time.

I reaffirmed why I enjoy leadership development. I thoroughly enjoy witnessing the "aha" moments with my clients. To see leaders shift their mindsets, learn new skills, and apply those skills in real-time is life-changing. Every one of us wants to be heard and understood. We all have had to embrace virtual workspaces and continue delivering on the business goals. I enjoy the interface with teams and helping them create high-performance cultures and seeking solutions on how best to navigate team goals. I am immensely grateful for all the clients and partners I get to work with in the leadership development space. It is gratitude that continues to propel me forward.

My vision statement helped me realize the importance of my values. According to the Oxford English Dictionary, values are "principles or standards of behavior; one's judgment of what is important in life."

If I simplified that definition, it would be that "value" is a way of believing or being that we uphold as our truth. Knowing those values that are important to you helps you determine what will be a career that brings you excitement and worth.

Values are quintessential to who you are as a leader and can have a positive impact on the team mindset. What do you stand for? In times of crisis, do you lean on your values? How would your team describe your leadership style when things are unsettling? When things are calm? Would I know your values when you walked into a room? Can your team articulate the company values? When your company needs to make a major decision, do your business decisions align with your core values?

Values-based leadership is the intersection of knowing your own leadership values and the values of the organization. Do your personal values align with your workplace values? Are the company's decisions rooted in the core values? When you lead and make decisions based on your values, you are leading from a place of transparency. It becomes very clear to others who you are and what you stand for. Let's explore a scenario. Think of a conversation that you had with a team member that may have caused you to react emotionally. Historically, you have responded in a not-so-positive way. Imagine responding based on your deepest value. Think about how different the outcome might be when you lead with your values. Realize your values and the importance of how they reflect how you lead.

The most important thing to remember about a team mindset shift is that when you are working on your vision, know your worth and lead with your values. What is it that you bring to the table that adds value to your team? What is it that you have yet to learn? A quote from Tene Edwards: "Know your worth—you must find the courage to leave the table if respect is no longer being served."[3]

Take deliberate steps daily to build your team value proposition.

As I state in *Aim High, Ask Why: Discover your Strengths*, I

---

[3] Quotespedia.org. (2020, July 11). *Know your worth. you must find the courage to leave the table if...* Quotespedia.org. Retrieved June 15, 2022, from https://www.quotespedia.org/authors/t/tene-edwards/know-your-worth-you-must-find-the-courage-to-leave-the-table-if-respect-is-no-longer-being-served-tene-edwards/.

believe it is still important to have an internal and external focus on your career. A suggested objective may be to obtain as much cross-functional experience as possible. Once you have established your vision, if you are interested in moving into a next-level position, most roles tend to have broad exposure across business functions as well as functional knowledge in specific areas. Steve Jobs said it best: "If you are working on something exciting that you really care about, you do not have to be pushed. The vision pulls you. Create a vision that makes you want to jump out of bed in the morning."

How are you moving toward your big, audacious goal, that ginormous "idea" that you must do? Writing down your leadership vision and leading with your values sometimes takes courage. What does courage look like to you? You might be terrified as you approach it, when you're working toward your goals, there's a peace, a sense of joy, of being in your "zone" that pulls you back to it time after time. You may consider seeking a coach to help you strengthen your courage muscle and carry out your leadership vision.

COACHING

In my first book, *Aim High, Ask Why*, I shared stories about my human resources experiences when I coached leaders on their career goals. I thought it was very important to share this section again because I continue to advise my clients that it has been helpful for me to have a mentor/coach on my career journey.

If you have ever found yourself wondering what coaching really is, or how it differs from mentoring, I will define what a mentor is and provide you with several examples of what coaching is and the different types of coaching.

A mentor is someone who helps guide you through your personal or professional journey. Mentors are typically available to offer advice, speak on your behalf in leadership meetings, and are someone you should seek out when you need an unbiased opinion. Having a mentor within your company can prove valuable.

They can identify opportunities for advancement you might have overlooked. A mentor can also guide you through challenging projects and help you build relationships with the senior management team. I have utilized a mentor many times in my profession to help me navigate my career. My mentors asked me questions that made me think about all options for my career aspirations. Questions such as: Who are the people of influence at the executive level that I need to meet? What position should I consider applying for next? What is my professional brand?

A coach is someone who has an impartial, yet supportive role in helping you meet your personal and professional goals. Let's use a car as an analogy. A car can go super fast, but only if the driver starts the engine and presses the accelerator. No one else has the keys to your car and you are the only one who drives it. The coach is like the passenger in your car, who helps you navigate your road trip based on insight from you.

Coaching helps bridge the gap between an adaptable and fulfilling career. Closing the gap is all about moving people from where they are now to where they ultimately want to be. However, the actual role of a coach is often misunderstood. Coaching is an inquiry-based process where the focus is centered on how to build awareness, create clarity, and develop actionable next steps. As the coach, I partner with you and hold you accountable for taking those actionable next steps. A coach is a true accountability partner. The coach is there to take the career journey with you. The International Coach Federation defines coaching "as partnering with clients in a thought-provoking and creative process that inspires them to maximize their personal and professional potential."

Coaching is an opportunity to explore, through powerful questions, how we are and how we think. How can I, as a coach, enable clients to reinvent their way of being and their way forward? When I coach, I co-create space that inspires and enables my clients to think differently about their own way of being and their way forward.

The coach will ask questions that will bring out what is already housed within you. They are not there to tell you what you should do next. The role of the coach is to ask pointed questions that will help you arrive at your own conclusions and encourage forward movement.

Coaching takes place through conversations. Regular communication using coaching conversations is essential. In fact, the single most important leadership competency that separates highly effective leaders from average ones is coaching.

Some of the questions that help my clients center their vision for the upcoming year reflect on the uncharted possibilities. Is the normal you have left behind the normal you want to return to? How will you make your new normal more of what you want it to be? How do you connect with an amazing group of like-minded professionals who share your passion for coaching, learning, and excellence?

Coaching can also be defined as partnering with clients in a thought-provoking and creative process that inspires them to maximize their personal and professional potential. A coach can help you develop a growth/coach mindset. A growth mindset is the ability to see and know what is possible. Whether it is changing careers, revamping your business strategy, or simply starting over, a coach can help you make the decision on how you want to elevate your business and professional roadmap. Write down your vision. Make sure your first draft leads to your final draft.

How can you have a coach mindset? A coach mindset focuses on strengthening your credibility and competence. Human resource business partners can help you build the competencies needed for coaching success by recommending leadership courses or projects that can help you maximize your leadership impact. Human resources can positively impact how leaders show up in their roles and ultimately shift the skill level upward in the organization. These HR colleagues can help senior executives develop greater self-awareness and refine their leadership behaviors in ways these leaders have rarely experienced.

Coaching can transform not only leader effectiveness it can also ensure a healthier company culture operating at a high-performance level.

I offer Group and Leadership Coaching and often the focus of those sessions is centered on the client wanting an accountability partner to make sure they are putting their personal values into practice and strengthening their leadership muscle. In 2020, I wanted to provide a forum for leaders to keep those muscles active. Many of my coaching clients were distracted and were very shaken not only by the pandemic but also the looming epidemic. As a result, in May of 2020, I offered free coaching sessions, entitled Calm Connection. My intention for this group coaching was to create a miniseries of coaching sessions where leaders could keep their personal vision top of mind and, more importantly, actively participate in a forum with like-minded business professionals and have their voices amplified. This was a space for leaders to share ideas on how to identify the next best steps in their careers. I soon realized that some of them were experiencing their own form of outward success and inward mess. On the outside, their careers seemed to be moving forward; however, when they were honest with themselves, they realized their inner happiness was lacking. Coaching individuals and teams on how to show up for themselves in a climate of ambiguity is challenging. It continues to be paramount to the coaching work I do.

The Calm Connection group coaching sessions were held monthly. We had discussions on how to show up with your true self and everyone around you. We spent a fair amount of time exploring how to make tough conversations easy within their teams. How do you rebuild trust when the team does not feel that leadership is modeling trust and transparency? You begin by having one conversation at a time. Meet with your manager about your concerns, even if it is uncomfortable. Brainstorm ways you can be a part of the solution. If needed, reach out to your coach and get their perspective on the best approach given your culture and environment. For example, when leadership asks the team for ideas on how to create more transformational leaders, you should be prepared to share your thoughts and ideas on what type of leadership support you need to be successful in your role. The most powerful questions come from deep, contextual listening which we can do more effectively when we are fully present. Don't wait for the meeting after the meeting with your friends or colleagues, share your thoughts today. Stay curious.

AGILE COACHING

In writing *Aim High, Ask Why*, I reflected on our complex, globalized, and technologically competitive business landscape, and how organizations are increasingly seeking ways to become more Agile. The benefits of this type of coaching are being able to manage shifting priorities, improving productivity, and leading with innovation. However, becoming Agile is an ongoing journey that requires courage, strength, and commitment.

When your strategy is to discover ways to unlock and foster agility in an organization, a specialized coach, such as an Agile coach, can play a critical role. However, the Agile coaching role is often inconsistent and poorly misunderstood.

So, what is an Agile coach? Agile coaches are servant leaders. In his book *Good to Great*, Jim Collins describes a servant leader as one who possesses a rare mix of humility and intense determination. In contrast with traditional leadership models, where people serve those above them, servant leaders personally invest their time, energy, and resources in developing the people who work for them. They hold a strong vision while largely decentralizing decision-making. The result is an organization composed of empowered, enabled leader-workers at all levels. And at the same time, execution happens faster since the people closest to the work are highly involved in the strategic process. When leaders coach their teams, it has significant positive effects on employee development, performance, and productivity (Source: Harvard Business Review, 2015).

There will be days when you are not feeling the career love.

The kind of love that makes you jump out of bed and race to your workplace. Okay, maybe you are not racing to work; however, you understand the excitement. So, I encourage you to be curious and dig deep. Even when you fall out of love, there is something you like about what you do. Build on those likes. Work your action plan. Your action creates clarity. If you have committed to working with a coach, honor your commitment to yourself. You are worth it. Questions you may think about as you work with a coach:

- What are your strengths?
- What are your development needs?
- For the coaching to be successful, what behavior changes need to take place?

The most important fundamental value of coaching is confidentiality. When clients enter a coaching relationship with me, they can be assured I hold our conversations in confidence. This trust factor has been a part of me throughout my HR career.

Coaching affords me the opportunity, through my questioning, to remain curious. The more open-ended the questions are, the more opportunity for in-depth dialogue. Again, remember my role is not to *solve* your concerns. It is to create a brave space for building a trusting relationship to help design the best path forward for you.

So how could you manage up? It is helpful to have a set of tools that you can quickly use to develop a shared purpose with senior leaders around your development that supports momentum and business-guided growth. You can help set the wheels in motion for leaders and HR partners to have deeper, more collaborative coaching discussions about what may be hindering their potential for greater leadership success.

You can also seek out a coach to help navigate your career path. As a coach, I get the opportunity to help individuals explore their authentic selves and devise an action plan to further define their career path forward. No one can walk your career path like you. As best as you can, get clarity on where you are headed next in your career.

Through coaching, is it possible to build trust with people even if we can only communicate over Zoom screens? YES! And YES! Given what we know about the workplace and the multiple disruptions and pandemics that have faced our country and the world, it couldn't be a more opportune time to seek out a coach, reinvent yourself, and build trusting relationships.

Investing in your employees' professional development creates the foundation for more effective, productive, and positive workspaces, whether those are in the office, virtual, or both.

Additionally, the workforce is rapidly changing and so are the demands on leaders to create a more diverse, virtual, and inclusive workplace. Business professionals must demonstrate new strategies, policies, and skills in order to be effective business partners. Likewise, they must also manage their own professional- and personal-life changes and navigate through the winds of change in this era of disruption.

Leaders are making decisions from a virtual Zoom space while navigating between the needs of the organization and the needs of those they lead. Let's take a Z.O.O.M. (Zoom In, Operating Guide, Optimism, Motivation) approach to walk through this process.

ZOOM IN

Inspired leaders focus on ways to help their teams:

- Build connection
- Create community
- Encourage collaboration

OPERATING GUIDE

As you work to build out the reimagined workspace, remember the vision that worked for your organization five years ago will not be the vision to take your team into the next five or ten years. What has this year/last year taught you about how best to lead the team in the future? Leverage the brainpower of your team to solve for why.

OPTIMISM

Create space for your team to further develop their strengths and focus on their leadership development needs. Utilize resources such as leadership assessments, podcasts, and executive coaching to inspire them to thrive.

MOTIVATION

Employee engagement can be increased by empowering individuals to flourish in the job you hired them to do. Additionally, ensure you are building trust, inviting curiosity, and inspiring them to rise to their potential.

One of the questions that I hear consistently from my clients and colleagues is, Where do I go from here? How do I motivate, adjust, and keep the business thriving and our employees focused on the vision? It starts with the choices you make that help the team carry out your vision.

Our choices reveal our intentions. What does it mean to be authentic? The dictionary defines authenticity as having a genuine original or authority; in opposition to that which is false. I believe authenticity is a choice. A choice to show up and be honest. A choice to be truthful.

Authenticity can be a delicate balancing act when you consider how the world may view what is real by the value we place on materialistic things. What authentic career choices do you need to make? Take a moment to answer these questions. What networks have you sought out on your leadership journey? What is your workplace culture leadership style? What has inspired you to move forward? What will be your legacy?

Networking is key. Do you enjoy networking events? Do you miss making professional connections? A collaborative culture focuses on coming together collectively, embracing new perspectives, and connecting with intentionality. Now is a great time to continue to build your networks. Now is the time to continue to reach out to your networks and share what you are working on and ask how you can best support your colleagues.

Additionally, you also want to focus on your external network because remember, networking is key. Think about those colleagues who either have the type of job you want or departments you would like to work in at some point in the future. Are there professional organizations or business social media platforms that can help you move your vision to your career of choice? How do you cultivate a career you love? One way is by creating space for networking, guided learning, and inspiration.

A Note to Leaders

Leaders, can I count on you to lead by example? Can I count on you to create a space that cultivates trust, embraces the vision, and inspires engagement while valuing differences? Can I count on you to play to the strengths of the team? Find out what each team member does well and create opportunities for each person to thrive. Remember, your direct report may or may not want your job. They want the position that is designed for them based on their strengths. Take time to get to know them. Don't make assumptions about what they enjoy about their role; just ask them. You can count on them to bring their strengths to the table, carry out the leadership vision, and ensure the success of the team. Can they count on you?

Career development comes down to
who can pivot in an ever-changing workplace.

CHAPTER TWO

NAVIGATING
YOUR CAREER PATH

As you navigate your career path, it will be important to recognize your strengths and development opportunities. Career development is a lifestyle. A lifestyle that includes deciding what you want to do next in your career with intentional focus. If you are searching, refreshing, or expanding your job search, it is important to define what is needed to reach the next level. Start from where you are. What is your superpower? Think about what specific accomplishments you are most proud of. Start thinking of how you will share those stories in a thorough and succinct way for a job interview. What are your career aspirations? What were some of your career-defining moments?

Discover your strengths. Knowing your strengths gives you a baseline of what capabilities and skill sets you bring to the table.

Strengths encompass the positive qualities of your leadership style. Ask yourself what do you do well? What expertise do your colleagues frequently request from you?

What are ways you can leverage your strengths as a leader? Know your top strengths. Consider completing a strengths assessment such as the VIA Character Strengths Survey, Strengths Finder, or Strengths Based Leadership to understand and align with your strengths. The Values in Action (VIA) Character

Strengths Survey measures twenty-four character strengths. Rather than focusing on what you "do" best, it is an assessment of who you are at your core. This assessment identifies what are your top strengths and how they link to your core values. It provides you with feedback on your strengths in rank order with the top five being your "signature strengths."

What are the critical focus areas of Strengths Based Leadership?

1. Know your top strengths and work toward using them daily. These are your leadership enablers.
2. The overuse of your strengths can cause you to lose sight of what you do well.
3. Get to know what motivates your staff. To lead people effectively you need to know who they are, what they value, their strengths, and the difference they want to make.
4. Ask your employees how you can best support them.

Another tool to help you identify your strengths is the StandOut Assessment, a free assessment offered by Marcus Buckingham, author of *Go Put Your Strengths to Work*. What is the StandOut Assessment? This brief assessment reveals your top StandOut Roles, the combination of traits that help you stand out at work. This assessment is designed to help you become more aware of where you are at your best. The results give you practical strategies for how to accelerate your performance.[4]

A strengths-based approach to leadership is a more effective way than the traditional method of just focusing on work performance weaknesses. To help organizations grow and thrive we need to tap into people's strengths.

Strengths-based leadership is an approach to leading others

---

[4] Buckingham, M. (2021, June 2). *Standout Strengths Assessment* . Marcus Buckingham. Retrieved June 15, 2022, from https://www.marcusbuckingham.com/gift-of-standout/.

that builds on what's strong, rather than what's wrong. Research and evidence-based best practices show that strengths-based leadership empowers leaders and the people who follow them and fosters healthy and positive workplace cultures.

In a constantly changing work environment, employees continue to face increasing levels of stress, change, and uncertainty. Disengagement, absenteeism, interpersonal conflict, lowered productivity, and turnovers are the unintended consequences when strengths-based leadership is absent. Under these conditions, it is not enough for leaders to simply be task-focused, running effective meetings and monitoring employee performance via Zoom. Today's leaders also need to think about how they engage, inspire, and develop their teams to be resilient and to flourish, despite the day-to-day challenges they might face.

Strengths-based leadership enables leaders to bring out the best in themselves and others by igniting their core character strengths. The focus on strengths is all about understanding and building on an individual's best opportunities for success. This approach does not discount that we need to understand and better manage our blind spots; however, it emphasizes the basic principle that individuals (and organizations) gain most when they build on their strengths rather than focus on their opportunities for development.

Great leaders do not have one single ingredient that makes them great. A consistent trait of great leaders is that they know their strengths and how to use them to become more influential.

Strengths-based leaders are self-aware, know who they are and what they value. They understand what their leadership enablers and derailers are and know how to manage these to get the best outcomes. They invest in their strengths, are clear on their leadership purpose, and know how to engage and influence others to follow their lead. They demonstrate fundamental traits around hope, optimism, confidence, and resilience.

Strengths-based leaders create the conditions for others to be successful. They do this by recognizing the strengths, talents, and skills of their employees. They lead by example, are transparent and authentic in their relationships with others, have strong guiding principles, are able to have a positive impact, and enable a workplace environment that supports people to reach their full potential.

Strengths-based leaders build trust, confidence, and followership by being true to who they are, fostering a positive environment, and being consistent in their leadership style and approach. They enable individuals to be more energized, engaged, and motivated to go above and beyond what is expected of them. Most importantly, they promote and align the best in others toward achieving optimal outcomes, performance, and organizational success.

How do you really know yourself? Self-awareness can enhance your career and fast-track your path to success. As you navigate your career path, consider the Strengths Based Leadership perspective: it is not enough just to know your strengths; it is also imperative to know your blind spots.

Blind spots are personal traits or aspects we may not even know about that may limit the way we act, react, behave, or believe, and therefore limit our effectiveness. Have you been told you are too critical? Impatient? Conflict-averse? Easily offended?

The biggest opportunity I have when I coach leaders in their careers is helping them identify what position they play on their team. For example, on any given project, you may not be the lead. For another assignment, your idea may not make it to the innovation table. The timing, the resources, or even your attitude may be the cause of the delay. Be curious. Find out what it is that you have yet to learn. It might not be your time to be in the starting lineup. On the other hand, the leadership team may be positioning you for another role based on the immediate needs of the business. It is important to remember the right position may not be your right now position. Stay focused and don't lose sight of the end goal.

Much research has supported the fact we all have blind spots.

In coaching with my clients, the blind spots that show up most often are:

- Avoiding the difficult conversations (conflict avoidance)
- Going it alone (being afraid to ask for help)
- Having an "I know" attitude (valuing being right above having peace)

Once you become aware of your blind spots, what is next? I have listed a few suggestions to get you started.

Solicit feedback. Ask a friend for feedback. "What is the one blind spot I have that I should be more aware of?" Or say to your friend, "A leadership assessment identified some unique blind spots. Do you feel there is one blind spot that shows up in how I approach things?" Surround yourself with colleagues who you can learn from. You recognized your blind spot; now decide how can you strengthen this development opportunity. Review your past performance to identify patterns.

How have you succeeded as a leader? How have you struggled? What situations have led to both desirable and undesirable outcomes? What feedback have you received from mentors, coaches, or advisors regarding decisions you've made that indicate a pattern of questionable choices?

Identify triggers. We all have triggers or situations that cause us to impulsively react without thinking. When we take control of our triggers, we own how we respond and make them work for us, rather than against us. Remember, when you are triggered, don't react; instead create space so you can respond in ways that align with your values.

Seek out an accountability partner. Once you've received feedback on your blind spots, enlist someone you trust to hold you accountable for behavioral change. Start with the feedback you have received to date. Is the feedback from your immediate manager? Colleague? Previous manager? The difference between who you are now and who you want to be in the future is what you do with the feedback you have received. It can all prove to be valuable information as you begin to navigate the next steps in your career.

Take time to reflect. What feedback have you received recently that you may have ignored? Write down and consider again if the feedback is worth acting upon. Use the feedback you have received from your performance reviews as another data point. If possible, seek out feedback from your peers such as the Leadership 360 Assessment. This is another feedback tool that provides information on your potential blind spots from your colleague's perspective.

What are those things that you cannot see that may be hindering your development? You are here for a purpose. Get out of your own way. People are waiting for you. Make sure you have put in the work to get the clarity to get moving.

Self-awareness is the ability to focus on yourself and how your actions, thoughts, or emotions do or don't align with your values. It is helpful to know how you are showing up in the workplace. Developing self-awareness allows leaders to assess their personal growth and change course as needed. I get it. Sometimes you may have multiple emotions showing up in multiple ways and it feels like an emotional roller coaster. When your emotions are triggered by a specific event or conversation, how do you respond? It is so important to know where your emotions are showing up in your body.

If you have strong emotions from childhood or previous events in your life, that trauma is not your fault. However, your healing and growth become your responsibility. You can choose if you want to work on those emotions or allow those old scripts to play in your head. Another option is to recognize the emotion and make a different choice by growing your choice muscles. Choice muscles give you options on how you will respond to a situation.

The first step was to identify the critical lessons of Strengths Based

Leadership from a Virtual Landscape, which includes discovering your strengths and your blind spots, now is the time to put those strengths to work and further develop your blind spots so you can rise to your potential.

How can you rise to your potential? Work on building your network/relationships. Who can you seek out on a conference call, or schedule a zoom meeting to get insight on how best to advance your career? What projects could you contribute to?

Your internal network should be those who you have helped or those who can help you navigate your career successfully. Get to know your colleagues. Find out what drives them. Discover what their interests are outside of work. Consider joining affinity groups or business resource groups at your company. It is a great way to further display your leadership talent and meet new people.

Your external network should be those connections you have made outside of your job. These will be some of your most lasting connections. Also, include who you want to add to your network and who can help you develop your professional growth. Maybe there is someone you know that could really help you turn your dream career into reality. Make a list of those people and invite them to have virtual coffee or conduct an informational interview with them. You can also reach out to communities of practice or seek out professional connections within your LinkedIn groups.

Networking gives you the opportunity to determine how someone can help you and how you can help someone else reach their goal. Make it a habit not to just help someone when you have free time, but free your time to help someone. Participate in organizations that can enhance your development. These organizations can be directly related to your career. When your schedule permits, be curious, and feed that curiosity by attending at least one conference a year to further enhance your professional development. Learn something every day about your field of interest. Join groups and follow hashtags and companies you would like to work for.

It is not about who you know, it's about who knows you. As you build your network/relationships:

- Be a resource; share resources with your team on how best to navigate change; recommend leadership books/podcasts.
- Be transparent; ask for what you need.
- Be vulnerable; move away from the desire to have it all together; show people you are human. We get better as a team when we trust one another.

Ask yourself, where are you investing your time, talent, and contributions?

Similar to Agile coaching mentioned in the previous chapter, the ability to navigate one's career with agility means more than appreciating strengths and development opportunities. It also requires an awareness of your interests, preferences, and values.

Agile navigators develop a lifestyle of A.I.M.ing high by being:

- Amazed—be aware of your gifts. How can you help others? Evaluate what contributes to (or distracts from) your career development. Find out what it is that you love and what nurtures you.
- Inspired—what causes you to become the most effective team player? Take time to journal and write down your goals.
- Motivated—examine ways that keep you improving your career development. Seeking feedback from others can help you when you don't see how you are showing up in the workplace.

Every previous position provides learnings that help you navigate your career path and reach success in your current position. You have learned lessons along the way. Each learning is an opportunity to gain strength and endure the next lesson.

What if you chose to shift your paradigm? Consider looking at your job as if you were there to serve others. Would you approach your day differently? Decide what motivates you.

How can you grow from where you are? You have demonstrated your ability and are clear on what skills you want to develop. You can move closer to deciding what it is you want to accomplish in your career. You cannot expect to succeed if you only put in the work on the days you feel like it. What are the projects or additional responsibilities that could position you for greatness? Remember you want to be successful and that takes putting in the work. What do you do with the career choices you make? How do you move from choice to success?

Once you have the answers to those questions, you are ready to create your career success statement. What does success look like to you? How will you feel when you reach your goals? What would you expect to see at this level? What do you need to do to sustain this level of career success? All of these questions can help you get the answers you need to design your career success statement. Are you making decisions and plans that will best prepare you for the career path you want to move toward?

Let's be honest. If someone would have told you there would be tough days ahead on your career path, you probably would not have ended up in your current role. Ask yourself, when things get tough, how do you stay resilient?

Many of us have taken the autopilot route to work. We get in our car or sign on to the conference call and somehow end up at our designation/meeting space. Just as you pull into the parking space or just before you turn on your conference call camera, here come the questions from your inner self: What else do I need to get or give to feel fulfilled in my role? How do I honor myself?

There will be times when you will question whether you are in the right position. When will all of your hard work pay off? Take the time to refine your craft, and this will ultimately create a better you. Try not to be concerned with people who do not have your best interest at heart. Surprisingly, there will be some colleagues that may question if you were ever qualified for the job. Are you up for the task to take your team to the next level? My best advice is to continue to show up with your best self. Immerse yourself with great insights and new perspectives. Challenge your own assumptions and grow as an individual and a leader.

When you reflect on your career path, where do you go or what do you do to refuel? No matter how hectic life gets, you should make time for yourself. So, you may ask, "How do I do that when there are not enough hours in the day?" Revisit your timeless traditions for reconnecting with yourself. You may want to start something new or expand the ways in which you unwind. You can begin by powering off all electronic devices. Go for the no-screen zone for one day. Plan a mini-vacay or staycation. Always take time to pause, take a deep breath, and if you need to step away, do that.

Sometimes the best thing you can do for yourself is to not think too hard about the stresses of life. How can you imagine the best possible outcome? Remember to breathe and know that everything will work out for the best.

When we feel strong emotions, especially negative emotions, it is easy to react to them rather than respond. Disappointment is a great example. Without even realizing it, disappointment can lead you to make decisions you wouldn't make otherwise.

Reacting instead of responding to disappointment could show up in many ways. For instance, maybe you didn't do a great job on a past project at work and feel like you are still paying the price for a mistake that happened months ago. Don't allow colleagues to continually remind you of your mistake. They should have some of their own mistakes to focus on.

These reactions could manifest in other ways for you, or it could be another strong emotion that's more likely to trigger that kind of "flight or fight" reaction. Whatever the emotional trigger is, there is a simple but effective tool that will help you respond logically and wisely instead of reacting. The first step, begin to name what you're feeling. Matthew Lieberman, a researcher at

UCLA, coined this method "affect labeling."[5] When you feel that little tinge of resentment, or another emotion, call it out. Say out loud, "This is disappointment." "This is fear." "This is resentment." Then pause, take a deep breath, and make the conscious decision that disappointment will not determine the actions or choices you make. What negative emotion tends to cause you to react with fear or drive your decisions off course? What emotion makes you say yes when you want to say no? What feelings keep you from speaking up when you should? What emotions have been causing you to react rather than respond positively?

Next time you feel that emotion rising, name it. Call it out, don't allow it to have control over your decisions. When you feel tempted to react, take a moment to exhale and think about how the wrong reaction can have negative consequences. The choices you make today impact your tomorrow. What's one thing you can do today that would make you proud? Then tomorrow, why not challenge yourself again? While navigating your career path, you will experience seasons of adversity. It helps to slow down, be intentional, and celebrate the wins. You're doing great. Just keep going.

A NOTE TO LEADERS

Check in with your team. Connect with each team member regularly and find out how they are doing and what support they need to make the best choices for themselves or their families. Don't wait until the next pandemic to express empathy toward your team members. A workplace that embodies strength-based teamwork is ideal. Everyone on the team plays to their strengths.

---

[5] Abblett, M., O'Leary, W., Smookler, E., Reicherzer, S., Cratsley, R. F., & Magee, R. (2022, January 18). *Tame reactive emotions by naming them.* Mindful. Retrieved June 15, 2022, from https://www.mindful.org/labels-help-tame-reactive-emotions-naming/#:~:text=Research%20has%20shown%20that%20mere%20verbal%20labeling%20of,in%20the%20brain%E2%80%99s%20emotional%20centers%2C%20including%20the%20amygdala.

Why? Because the coach, the leader, knows what each team member does well. You also know the projects they enjoy. How do you know this? They have demonstrated their stellar performance in the workplace. You have engaged them in performance discussions. The performance reviews have highlighted all their accomplishments, and these were discussed throughout the year. Now is the time to play to the team's strengths. Make it your priority to know the strengths of your team. It is your responsibility to know how everyone on the team can contribute to the success of the team. What is each team member capable of doing and what are the opportunities for them to further develop and grow? It is important as a leader of a team or a project to know the strengths of your team. Effective leaders allow great people to do the work they were born to do.

There is no direct path to your career destination.

CHAPTER THREE

SUPPORT ON
YOUR JOURNEY

Journeys are bittersweet . . . it's the mistakes, the rough roads, the missed turns that end up shaping our lives. Learning from life's speedbumps, are worth the journey. Take a moment to reflect on your current career journey. Have you ever found yourself with a great job working with good people? You followed the path you thought you were supposed to, based on your education and background. As you progressed in your career, you realized you have learned a lot and were given bigger responsibilities. You felt respected by your colleagues and were considered the go-to person. As days and months went by, you began to feel overwhelmed and frustrated. You may have even felt like everything was on your shoulders, and there was no relief in sight. And here's the thing: most of the "work" you were working on wasn't providing meaningful value to you. More and more, you began experiencing a growing friction, an internal resistance. You spent an enormous amount of time in meetings where the outcome was to schedule another meeting. Does any of this sound familiar?

You may also find yourself on the other end of the career spectrum, which is a career full of excitement. You feel privileged to work alongside some of the most talented colleagues and leaders. They have become lifelong friends and mentors.

As you move along your career path, you will encounter times similar to these or come to a fork in the road and want to do something different in your career. When you decide it is time to pivot, you will need support on your journey. This statement is still so true today as it was when I wrote my first book, *Aim High, Ask Why.* Today's multifaceted business environment continues to force disruption within and across organizations, including career development. Having a clear picture of what motivates you, who can help you, and how you develop professionally can prevent missteps in your career.

If you have a desire to keep learning, career leaps are par for the course. Career leaps are when you take chances, volunteer for new projects, make mistakes (and learn from them) and most importantly, make the decision to have fun along the way.

Let's start this next career journey by identifying what types of actionable commitments, leadership support, and professional development experiences you will need along the way. Commitment ignites action. To commit is to pledge yourself to a certain purpose. It also means practicing your beliefs consistently. There are two fundamental conditions for commitment. The first is having a core set of beliefs. The second is an alignment of your beliefs with your behavior. Possibly the best description of commitment is "persistence with a purpose."

Day to day, commitment is demonstrated by a combination of two actions. The first action is called supporting. Genuine support develops a commitment in the minds and hearts of others. This is accomplished by focusing on what is important and leading by example. The second action underlying commitment is called improving. Improving is a willingness to look for a better way and learn from the process. It focuses on eliminating complacency, confronting what is not working, and providing incentives for improvement.

Be diligent about maximizing your leadership performance. Navigate as needed around the career delays and shifts in promotions and demotions. Sometimes you may need to take one step forward and two steps back to position yourself for your next move. Drive your own leadership development. Discovering new development opportunities such as formal (online workshops, webinars, and e-learning) to informal (development experiences, mentoring, visibility, and networking) are ways to drive your own professional development. It also means being willing to adjust your career action plan and seeking support from your peer and team squad.

What is a peer squad? A peer squad is a group of people you can count on when important events happen in your life. How could your peer squad support you in your career today? Just like when a rocket takes off from the launch pad, there is a team of people inside command central who are there to help ensure the takeoff and landing are successful. Peer squads are the people you can call on when faced with day-to-day life challenges, when you are puzzled by a manager's decision, or when you need space to be seen and heard. You may ask them for their insight and ideas, their point of view, or for feedback and encouragement. The members of your peer squad were not voted into these positions. They may not even know they are a part of your peer squad. However, you know they have been critical to your career success and your mental well-being.

There are usually a core group of people who have consistently supported you in your career. The first group is your personal self-motivating cheering section. Sometimes you must be your own cheerleader. Think about all the ways you cheer yourself on. So, if you find yourself hiding behind the fear that things just might not work out, make a shift to focusing on this opposite question: What if it does work out? Fear dresses up as doubt, procrastination, or even scarcity. Fear can stop us in our tracks and derail us from our career goals. Whether it's the job you want, a business you want to open, or the retirement you have been longing for, remember you always have a choice. A choice to dismiss these thoughts and walk away or take on these thoughts, look them square in the face, and rise to your potential. Now is not the time to let fear rule your emotions or your decisions. Now is the time to be intentional to overcome your fear with affirmation and determination.

We are what we continuously tell ourselves along this journey. We are great, we are important, we matter, and we can do whatever we put our minds to do. It is in our walk, our talk, our actions, and even how we view ourselves. Who do YOU see when YOU look in the mirror? You should see greatness! You are uniquely and wonderfully made.

While you take steps along the journey, leave affirmation footprints to support yourself. Affirmations are centered around re-reading the positive notes you have on your bathroom mirror. You know, those notes that tell you to keep going. The notes that affirm you are enough. You may even have your favorite quote on your smartphone. Have you considered setting your Spotify playlist to include all your favorite sing-along songs to get you excited about your next BIG step? As you move toward your next BIG step, extend yourself some self-compassion. Where have you been too hard on yourself for missing a deadline or not taking that next BIG step? I will always encourage you to trust your gut and take steps, large or small, to align your priorities with your career choices.

An important step that will help you build your confidence is to first acknowledge that times may be harder today than usual. If things feel tough, stressful, or difficult right now, take a moment to say to yourself, "This is not easy. This is stressful." Do your best and let that be enough. Try to reduce your stress level and collect your thoughts on how to move forward.

If you start to feel as though your workload is too much, one of the actions you can take is to start setting boundaries. The ability to say "no" or "not now" is a gift to yourself and to others. Your heart may think yes, but your time says no. Grant yourself permission to no longer be the superhero. No need to add one more thing to your plate that is already full. Being all things to all people is and continues to be an unrealistic mindset. Ask for the help and support you need.

The other career cheering section is #TeamLevelUp. You can fill in the blank with your favorite hashtag. For me, it is #TeamLevelUp. This cheering section is similar to the television show *Who Wants to Be a Millionaire* or *Cash Cab*. On these television shows, a contestant is given the chance to phone a friend to answer a question to keep them in the game. The key to advancing to the next level is making sure you select a friend who can help you come up with the correct answer to stay in the game.

Your #TeamLevelUp cheering section includes the first person you call when you have exciting news. Who holds you accountable when you say something wrong? More than likely, it is your #TeamLevelUp Squad. This core group of people has a vested interest in your success. They are not in competition with you. They are not threatened by you. They genuinely want to see you succeed and want to know what they can do to help you get there.

Your #TeamLevelUp squad can help you think through why an idea would not work. This squad will also help you with the what-if questions. "What if" my dream does not work out the way I planned? Will I still be okay? Have you ever imagined your biggest dreams not working out? I have imagined myself reaching the finish line and brainstormed ideas on how my dream may not turn out as planned. I also realized the world would not come to an end. It is okay to have a big dream while at the same time considering a plan B. When I allowed myself to consider other options, it took some of the pressure off to succeed and helped me let my dream play out as it was designed. As you look back over your career, every time you thought you were being denied or rejected from a great position, you were really being redirected to something better.

What if your career dreams turned into reality? Lean on your #TeamLevelUp squad for the hope you need on your journey. Hope takes courage. It means believing in a possibility that just might come true. If the idea of being disappointed feels too uncomfortable, it's possible you'll quit hoping altogether. Hope is necessary for building and living out your dreams because it empowers you to persevere toward your most authentic career goals.

Support on your journey with the #TeamLevelUp squad could also include your previous/current manager. Take a moment to think about the leaders who have had a positive impact on your career. What do you remember most about their leadership traits? The first leader who comes to my mind always led by example. I remember how she developed us as leaders. She rolled up her sleeves and ensured we met our HR monthly deliverables. She also inspired me to set stretch goals. It was my personal career goal to become the Vice President of Human Resources and she was instrumental in making that happen for me. She spoke my name in rooms that I was never in and believed in me from day one.

Most of us are doing what we love and loving what we do at work. We want to continue to grow and develop. Sometimes we come to a bump in the road. Continue to find the best environment to showcase your talents. Remember to stay positive. Find the good in a bad situation by modeling the behavior you want to see. Do not allow anyone to zap the positive energy out of your day. Stay true to you. Make a conscious decision to keep your energy at the highest level. Decide what are the things that bring you sustainable happiness. Create career-defining moments. It is never too late to be what you might have been. There are so many ways to reinvent yourself and make positive changes and be all that you want to be. As you seek support in your career, think about how you can help support others.

As you reflect on the support you need on this career journey, where do you start? Think about what you enjoy doing. Who can assist you with a mind-mapping exercise? Mind mapping allows you to capture possible options you can take on your career path. You can also capture who you will need while you are on your way to success.

As you explore other career options, and if money or resources were not a factor, would this be the career you would choose? Write down all the possibilities on how this next phase of your career could come to fruition. Remember these are the first steps you can take to refine what possible outcomes you want to pursue. Try not to overthink this step. Your end goal is to get clarity on what will help you move closer to your goal. Based on the results from your mind map, there may be many options. For now, just start with career option number one. Then decide what you will do today to bring you closer to your career goal. What action steps can you start taking today?

- Create your own personal career playbook. The playbook should include short-term and long-term goals focused on your professional development. Establish a routine of capturing key actionable steps you will take daily to reach your weekly and monthly goals.
- Design your G.O.A.T. vision board which includes the greatest of all-time career options you want to pursue. Cut out pictures and words from magazines or from Pinterest that visually depict where you are in your career and where you want to go. Be descriptive as possible on this vision board. What type of career will bring you the most joy? What is your work location? How much money will you make? By when? What will your support group look like?
- Ramp up your accountability. Seek out a tried-and-true accountability partner. This person could be a friend, colleague, or even a career coach. The role of the accountability partner is to support you on your journey and help you remain focused on key career milestones.
- Join a mastermind group. This is a group of like-minded business professionals who have their own individual goals and collaborate with other business professionals by offering support on their

journey. These ambassadors meet as needed with the intention of inspiring one another to reach their individual career wins.

- Schedule a monthly call with your coach. Set aside time to check in with your coach to discuss your early wins and potential roadblocks you may encounter as you drive toward your goals.
- Create a motivational career podcast. I have the perfect title: Make Your Move Monday. This would be a forum to share tips on key moves you will make each week to move you closer to your goal. It could also include interviews with influencers in your field of interest.

Support for your career can also come in the form of professional development experiences to inspire employee engagement, elevate leadership skills and capabilities, and drive bottom-line results.

Leaders can inspire employee engagement by investing and supporting the teams' professional development growth in ways that take their careers to the next level. Here are some suggestions to begin the dialogue:

- Meet with employees and have a meaningful conversation about their aspirations and professional development goals.
- Identify a hot topic that would be beneficial to the team. Empower a team member to lead the discussion.
- What if you could only recommend one book on leadership? What would you recommend? This is a great way to model the behavior you want to see in the team.
- Continue to allocate funds to cover the cost of external professional development experiences.

Make sure these are impactful development opportunities, not a random two-day conference, where the team can grow and learn.

- Work with each employee to identify one internal developmental activity/project that he or she might like to engage in, and then create a plan to make it happen.

With this approach, leaders create meaningful career-development experiences, enhance leadership skills, and deliver on their people-development strategies.

Everyone needs a team of people and supporters along the way. The next few sections outline the many supporters who want to see you take your career to the next level. Supporters such as a wellness partner.

Your wellness partner helps to make sure you take care of yourself. They remind you that self-care is the best care. You can count on them to encourage you to pause and schedule "me" time.

Another career supporter is your connector. This person is visible on all social platforms and believes their life purpose is to bring people together and connect them. The connector is usually the liaison between you and your next career opportunity. They introduce you to people in your profession or designated industry, in person or virtually. The connector also supports you by sharing your successes with others who could benefit from your wealth of knowledge.

Don't forget you can seek out peer-to-peer support.

- Help a peer complete their deliverables by providing information needed for the project, making introductions to contacts, and giving endorsements in meetings.
- Create a trusted space where a peer can share (personal/professional) what is on their mind.
- Communication with intention. Schedule meetings focused on career development.

All of these supporters on your career journey take ownership for creating and engaging in intentional relationships with you. They have helped you, inspired you, and helped to accelerate your learning year after year.

These supporters can also help you see that while parting is never easy, sometimes life presents new opportunities, and you need to let go of the old to pursue new goals. Remember what you have done well. The hardest part about leaving anything, especially your career, is leaving your comfort zone. You have to release what no longer serves you. Sometimes you must let go of what you are familiar with so you can take the needed risk to pursue the career you always dreamed about. Don't forget to take notes and be grateful for what you have learned along the way.

A NOTE TO LEADERS

It is no longer the senior leadership's job to take command and control. Instead, it should be to cultivate and demonstrate how to lead with trust and compassion. Leaders, please do not forget to check on your team members. Leaders ensure hard-working people are supported, rewarded, and appreciated. Take time to celebrate the wins. Ask your team members how they like to be recognized. When was the last time you thanked someone on your team? Celebrations can range from a thank you note to a paid day off toward a long weekend. Don't forget that gratitude is one of the biggest retention tools you have in your leadership toolbox.

When you feel like you don't have time to pause,
that's exactly when you most need to pause.

CHAPTER FOUR

TAKING BREATHS ALONG THE WAY

One of the simplest ways for evaluating where you are, where you want to be, or clarifying what has you stuck is to pause and take a breath. A pause, you know, that sacred space between your thoughts and actions. Life moves so quickly, and we usually want answers fast, but the only way to get clarity is to slow down, trust the process, expand your emotional intelligence, and take a deep breath.

The slowdown of life has given me the opportunity to be thankful for those things I lost in 2020 and 2021. What I didn't know, and wish someone would have told me, is that the sense of loss that I felt was a real emotion and normal. Losing the ability to enter a store to purchase groceries due to COVID was a real experience. Thankfully, I had the simplicity of sunshine and blue skies that helped me to recenter my focus by breathing and staying present. Slowing down to appreciate the small things was looking me right in the face. I was grateful for my virtual clients and even more grateful when deadlines got pushed back two additional weeks. We were all trying to sort out these major life event changes. Keeping the little things in perspective can help you make sure they don't become big things. It is important to slow down, take a breath, and enjoy the moment you have right now. Those deep breaths lead to whole-hearted connections.

Simon Sinek recommends using the "pause" approach. As a leader, your team will typically carry out what you need them to. However, if you "pause" and encourage the team to share their ideas first, you create opportunities for different opinions to emerge. Pausing is where learning happens. You become empowered and now have choices.[6]

What is your inner voice telling you? The inner voice is that conversation that goes on in your mind that wants you to decide whether you should go left or should you go right? This voice can be negative or positive. How do you calm down the inner voice when it speaks loud and only has negative thoughts?

Do you make time for quiet? In the rush of the day or the speed of the night, do you get quiet? When was the last time you listened to the birds sing or paid attention to your breath? Take those quiet times to make decisions and ask yourself the hard questions about your career.

Quiet time also allows you space to mentally plan the day ahead or reflect on a day's journey. You may be thinking, there is not enough time in the day or night to be quiet. I might tend to agree with you. However, I know we all have the same twenty-four hours in a day.

In your career, you will encounter problems as often as you breathe. When faced with a major challenge at work and in life, refocus and maximize what is important in your life at that very moment. When you can control the controllables and intentionally set aside time to just be quiet, you are probably more compassionate and hopeful about the day ahead, starting with this A.B.C. approach: the Acknowledge, Breathe, and Consider approach.

Acknowledge: What specific emotions are taking center stage in your mind? Be honest about those emotions and channel your

---

[6] Facebook. (n.d.). Retrieved June 15, 2022, from https://www.facebook.com/simonsinek/posts/embrace-the-pause/10156607324776499/.

positive energy. How will you ensure that kind thoughts stay at the forefront of your mind? Identify a word, phrase, or picture that calms you.

Breathe: Take a moment to take a breath. Don't take your breath for granted. Start practicing before you begin your day and make it a learned routine. When the flow of your day starts to get out of sync, practice intentional breathing.

Consider: What will you consider as your next best move after you have acknowledged your emotion and taken that next breath? Capture your answer to that question in your journal or keep it top of mind. Send yourself a positive text message. What is the one step you will take to move forward?

So, what now? The inner voice is often a cause for pause. The pause allows you time to consider all options. When faced with a decision, such as taking on a new project, expanding your business, taking on a new role, or reevaluating your workspace, remember YOU are worthy! You are enough! Go back to the inner voice A.B.C.s, silence the negative thoughts in your head, and move forward. You get to decide which inner voice serves you the best.

Self-care should be your priority and a self-declared luxury. If self-care is an opportunity for you to focus on what your mind and body need most, why don't you take better care of yourself? How often do you put your needs at the bottom of the list?

While the past two years have brought us all challenges we could have never anticipated, it may have caused you to question your next career move. Your values and priorities probably have shifted. I hope you took advantage of the 2020/2021 world halt and inserted yourself on your calendar. The pandemic forced many things. My hope is that you continue to be intentional about your time.

Staying resilient and being successful requires intentional self-care. When you're constantly putting out energy toward your responsibilities, challenges, and goals, you have to be conscientious about how to replenish that energy. How can you incorporate more rest into your schedule? Who do you need to connect with to feel energized? How could you intentionally disconnect from work this week to give yourself a break?

PACE YOURSELF

Take it ONE day at a time.

One of the things I love to do is to take walks early in the morning. It has been the calmest part of my day. Each day I walk a little more than the day before. One day, I decided I would add a jog to my morning routine. Well, on that day, that was not the best idea for me. What did I learn from that experience? I did not pace myself. Moving at one pace does not immediately advance you to the next.

When I think about my career path and virtual workspace, I am reminded this is a journey, not a sprint. Getting in my car to contend with traffic seems to be a thing of the past. The face-to-face interactions with my clients have turned into multiple Zoom conference calls. I go between wanting to get back to the days of moving so fast to wishing the world would slow down. I have now embraced that my new virtual workspace includes coaching my clients and facilitating workshops virtually. The days of the week, which at one time seemed to move at a snail's pace, are now moving faster from month to month. Calm can be a contagious energy. When leading change, are you calm and focused or anxious and scattered?

Patience is also important when you consider everyone handles change differently. Change often opens up new experiences and opportunities.

When I go against the pace of life, it requires so much energy. When I accept things for what they are, my breath has more of a rhythm. I insert calmness into my life when the pace of life seems to move too fast.

Reading provides a sense of calm for me. I read to widen my perspective on varied topics. These days, my quiet time is spent reading a lot. I did not know that world health and social unrest would enter my life the way that they did. When I read and take my quiet time, I am reminded of how I can retreat to calm and remain quiet amid all the noise. I hope you create quiet time for yourself and realize there is so much more to learn.

You can't pour from an empty cup. Eventually, your calm energy will run out. Make sure you fill yours first.

Below are some thoughts on how to embrace a less stressful life:

- Before your day ends, review your schedule for the next day. Are there documents you need to prepare? Do you have the conference call information included on your calendar?
- Create boundaries by scheduling time for distractions, such as checking emails, social media, and returning non-scheduled phone calls.
- Identify your "must-complete" goals for the year and prioritize them by levels of importance.
- Create a daily or weekly calendar that includes time for work, family, learning, and rest.

CENTER YOURSELF

The start of a new week, the middle of the month, or the start of another year requires centering yourself. This reflection time may be exciting for some and cause much anxiety for others. Find ways to center yourself. There are so many distractions and yet there are so many moments that take our breath away. What is it that you are to learn about yourself during this time?

Find your breath and breathe. It is so important for you to center yourself on what is really important. What is in your control? What is beyond your control? Self-care gives us all an opportunity to focus on what our mind and body needs most. What would your mind and body say about how to remain calm? My mind gets really calm when I look at the sky or observe the movement of the trees. When taking time away, give yourself permission not to be helpful. Find something unproductive to do that causes your mind and your body to be still and decompress. When was the last time you connected with nature? Or took some alone time? These are all ways in which you stay centered. Surround yourself with people who demand your mental wellness and healing and provide space for you to receive it. How else might you center yourself? Pause.

Why pause? Pausing invites us to suspend any negative thoughts and consider other perspectives. So, I invite you right now to take a moment with me and pause. Take a deep breath. Allow your mind time to consider the ways you can better use your free time, and how you want to show up in your relationships.

Then ask yourself, "Am I spending my time on the people and things that matter most to me?" Whether you answered yes or no to that question, take time to pause and take note of the situations in your life that are trying to get your attention.

What's got you stressed? What's got you running in circles? What problem has become even more difficult because of the way you've responded? Whatever it may be, take a moment to just breathe. Deep breathing lowers your blood pressure and helps you center yourself and gather your thoughts so that you can do what needs to be done, say what needs to be said, press forward, and be resilient.

As you take the needed breaths in your career, also take time to think about what type of leader you want to be. Are you an empathetic leader who has a genuine interest in the well-being of your team? When you take a moment to reflect on your answer to that question, what leadership traits do you think help leaders lead with empathy and compassion?

Through many conversations I have had with leaders, there are two key traits that empathetic leaders embody, and they are trust and self-awareness. Think about the people who have had a positive influence on your personal/ professional career. What was it that made them stand out for you? Did they have high emotional intelligence (EQ)? Emotional intelligence is about recognizing behavioral triggers and handling those situations objectively, thus resulting in developing strong connections with team members. Leading with emotional intelligence is when leaders desire to equip their team with all it takes to thrive and not merely survive. It has been proven that individuals are more productive when they are supported, trusted, and given the autonomy to grow to their potential. Most leaders that I coach have shared that trust was foundational to building any of their professional relationships.

Personal or professional, trust is integral to the success of that relationship. The way we behave either builds trust or destroys it. When trust is absent from a team, you can expect team members to:

- Hide their mistakes or weaknesses
- Not ask for help when needed
- Assume the worst and not positive intent
- Talk about one another instead of talking to each other

Empathetic leaders are open and honest. It is so much easier to remember the truth than keep up with an untruth. You can strengthen relationships with your colleagues when you ask for help when you need it. Especially if you are not judged because you asked for help. Leaders that do what they say they will do also build trust among the team. Be true to your word, and if you can't deliver, let the person know, ahead of time, not at the last minute. Lastly, trust-building behaviors must be consistent and ongoing. Your actions proceed you and knowing I can trust you strengthens relationships exponentially.

Self-awareness is so important in today's workplace where more leaders are working remotely, communicating digitally, and navigating collaboratively. Self-awareness is knowledge about your strengths, weaknesses, personality traits, communication, leadership styles, and emotional intelligence. It is both how you perceive yourself and an understanding of how others see you. Self-awareness requires a mindset that is curious and open to learning about yourself as a means of personal development. Self-awareness empowers a person to see themselves through a different lens, manage their emotions, ask for what they need, and respond more effectively. The underlying learning is helping people approach situations with curiosity and encouraging them to see others with self-compassion and appreciation.

A Note to Leaders

One way you can strengthen your emotional intelligence is by using a tool called a Leadership Shield. This tool is a visual way to explore how you came to your current position as a leader and what traits helped you get there.

Change requires a steady leader. Steady means consistently showing up with truth and patience. The team should trust that while you remain calm, you will share necessary updates as it relates to the company. It is also okay as a leader to feel as if things are falling apart. Learn ways to reset and recharge and extend yourself grace.

Expand your capacity as a leader to maximize the potential of your team through coaching them toward success. Learn how to develop trusting relationships in spaces where trust is core to the foundation. Trust your employees to make smart decisions about how and where they can have the greatest impact on achieving the company goals.

What would your day be like if you took a deep breath and showed up with empathy? When we choose to bring our authentic selves to work, we invite space for those around us to share in the joy, self-care, and compassion in our lives.

Invest in your career now so,
when later shows up, you are prepared.

CHAPTER FIVE

LIVE AND LEARN

Here is where I will refer to why I wrote this book. Simply stated, I wrote *Navigating Your Next Career Move* to inspire leaders to be curious about how to rise to their potential. I wanted to create space for business professionals to learn from my experiences while creating their own experiences. After a decade of managing and leading people in my own career, I have built my company, Essence of Coaching, around what I love, executive coaching and leadership development for business professionals. At Essence of Coaching, we inspire leaders to see the best inside themselves and take action steps to get there.

I am also the author of *Aim High, Ask Why: Discover Your Strengths, Uncover Your Blind Spots, and Rise to Your Potential*. I believe you have so much to offer the world when you use your knowledge and expertise. Let's explore some of the ways you can begin to do just that.

The concept of leadership is not new. What has evolved over time is the way in which we work and how we show up as leaders. I will share with you three leadership lessons that I have found to help good leaders become great leaders as well as specific resources you can begin using today.

Before we dive in, I want you to think about a leader who has had a positive influence on your career. Now, think specifically about what strengths this person held to make them a great leader.

- Were they trustworthy?
- Did that person empower you?
- Were they able to insert humor into your work life?

As a transformational leader in this virtual landscape using the three leadership lessons, Strengths, Blind Spots, and Rising to your Potential, will help you navigate your team's career path. Let's start with Strengths.

Leaders have a huge opportunity and responsibility to ensure new and existing employees know their strengths and use their onboarding plan or individual development plan to track progress in building their leadership muscle. These plans help to foster employee engagement and ensure a continued alignment of company goals and an employee's values. Use development plans in tandem with performance management and succession planning to continually reskill and upskill the leadership gaps.

First, managers need to keep in mind that growth plans should match their direct reports' career goals. Different employees have different aspirations, and the individual development plan isn't going to drive lasting results without the employees' buy-in. Next, managers and their direct reports should meet to identify specific strengths and career aspirations. Using a development plan makes this easier because it can guide the discussion. This plan should include steps on how and when the goal will be completed such as a commitment to lead a major project or enroll in a course on people management by the third quarter of the planning year.

The one-on-one meetings help keep your employee's strengths and development opportunities in focus by reminding the manager of the growth areas and progress. Secondly, it's a way to surface obstacles that your employee may encounter along the way.

The trend used to be that companies would have career conversations only once a year, perhaps during a performance review.

However, when you schedule shorter, more frequent meetings throughout the year, there is more opportunity to keep professional development moving forward. I encourage managers to have development conversations during their one-on-ones on a monthly or quarterly basis and continue making development conversations a priority year-round.

So, you have identified your Strengths and taken the time to go put them to work. You uncovered your Blind Spots and are more aware of how you are showing up in the workplace. So how do you manage your Blind Spots so they don't become a roadblock to you moving your career forward?

As referenced in chapter 2, Blind Spots are often seen as barriers for leaders who are not self-aware. Blind Spots should not stop your career; however, you have the opportunity to work on removing the barrier and deciding how the Blind Spot could become a potential Strength. How are you viewed among your peers? Do you want to change their perspective? Is there an opportunity for your mentor/coach to help you consider options and not let this be a career-ending obstacle?

Once you've made the decision on which Blind Spot you want to focus on, lean on your team squad, coach, and manager to help you make the necessary changes for your career development.

So, how do you begin to take the two leadership lessons and build on the third leadership lesson, Rising to your Potential? Let's start with LinkedIn, today's leading business professional platform. When was the last time you updated your profile? Are you fully utilizing it and showcasing your strengths? You want to make sure you are establishing your voice and crafting a leadership narrative that attracts the audience you are seeking. This is a social platform where you want to optimize your career profile and actively engage with other LinkedIn business professionals.

The next level of leadership competencies needed for 2022 and beyond will vary based on business trends and customer demands. Do you have the skills to advance to the next level of leadership? Are you consistently assessing your relevance and advancing your skills and capabilities to Rise to your Potential?

Have you researched what knowledge, skills, and certifications will be most in demand for your career? How are you continuing to grow and develop yourself so you get noticed when new opportunities become available?

Sharing more wisdom from the *Aim High, Ask Why* summary page, which states, if you can be anything in the world, be inspired. Inspired means to make someone want to do something: to give (someone) an idea about what to do or create. What inspires you? Where do you get your energy to jump-start your to-do list?

Often, we get so consumed with what's next that we forget about our current successes. What have you done this year? Last year? What were your accomplishments and achievements?

Also, think about: What did you learn in the past year? Why are you grateful? What time wasters did you have?

What virtual networking or professional events did you attend that were totally worth it? When did you have the most fun at work? What books are on your reading list? What professional development events do you want to attend? What training programs are you interested in?

The way we work has changed, and the need for team cohesion is so needed, now more than ever. A team can be defined as a group of people with a shared identity who collaborate to achieve a common goal. Each member should have the opportunity to make a contribution based on the strengths and diverse perspectives they bring to the table. Organizations tend to go down a rabbit hole of groupthink. You know, that space where team members stop thinking independently, don't speak up, and move quickly toward consensus? Teams unknowingly rate their sense of belonging in the group over the quality of the group's decision-making. One way to move the group to a cohesive team is to start with clarifying values, mission, goals, roles, and responsibilities.

Give yourself permission to reboot your career development

right now. How do you gain clarity around your blind spots that move you toward growth, learning, and performance improvement? You may feel some discomfort and need to get clear what is the source of that discomfort. Then listen to the inner guidance that tells you to make changes as needed. Some changes may be big, some changes will be small, and others may be mindblowing.

Remember, there is no direct path to your career destination. However, take a moment to envision yourself at the next destination. Understanding where you are now in your career is just as important as understanding where you are going.

What is the future that you have always dreamed of? Challenge yourself to do more than just dream about your future. Work hard to make sure it comes true. If you knew you could not fail, what would you choose to do with your life? Weigh your options. Build on all the things mentioned in this book and put your action plan together. An action plan includes the steps you will take to help you reach your career goal(s).

Give your goals the chance to succeed by making them S.M.A.R.T. goals: Specific, Measurable, Attainable, Realistic, and Timely. Designing your goals with a S.M.A.R.T. mindset, helps you get clarity on what you want to do versus what you will actually do. Check your current goals against the S.M.A.R.T. approach listed below.

Specific: There are numerous paths you could take to reach your career destination. To get yourself moving, decide on one or two goals to begin your journey. Consider what it will take to reach the goal. Try to narrow the focus of the goal. A broad goal is similar to when someone gives you vague directions. Eventually, you will get there. However, you realize there was probably an easier route.

Measurable: How will you know you have reached the goal? You have options. When possible, you want to apply metrics to your goals. Remember anything worth doing well usually involves assessing progress along the way. Sometimes the metrics are numerical. For example, you may decide you want to increase your sales goals by 10 percent. Another approach may be to consider the impact of the goal. When I complete this goal, I should expect a certain outcome. Lastly, you may want to focus on building a system and developing a process, rather than trying to achieve a goal or outcome.

Attainable: When you set your goal, will you achieve it? Is the goal so far-fetched that it is more of a wish or dream than an actual goal?

Realistic: Give your goals a reality check. I believe in dreaming big. I also believe I can dream bigger goals for myself. Is that a practical approach?

Timely: What is the time frame for completing the goal?

I challenge you to get more specific. When possible, identify the month and year. To help you get started, think of a time when you were at your best and reached a meaningful goal. What did you do to reach the goal? What did you learn about yourself along the way? What people or resources were important parameters to help you make it to the end?

Now think about a time when you did not reach a goal. What caused the disappointment? Were there specific distractions you should have removed from your innovation space? What did you learn from that experience that you do not want to repeat? Don't allow regret to be your constant companion. You have learned from it, now make a different decision.

Capture your smart goals in a notebook or template. Identify a place where you can readily access them and update your progress as needed. If you are not goal-crushing, then what are you doing? Taking your career to the next level means being willing to stand in uncomfortable places to experience your growth at extraordinary levels.

The love of your career can be endless. If you do not like the word love, replace it with passion. Whichever word you decide to use, remember anything worth keeping requires some level of work. Congratulations, you have put in the long hours, attended numerous Zoom meetings, scheduled team appreciation forums, and hopefully can see the fruits of your labor. Your good days will outweigh your bad days. You will soon come to realize YOU are making a difference. You are helping others see themselves in a different light. While the love may not always be reciprocated, keep doing the right thing. Your legacy will last beyond your current position.

That brings me to another point regarding leadership lessons. What do you want your legacy to be? This is something you should take time to reflect on and think about. You are a valuable resource to the company. What do you want to be known for? What is the impact you have provided to the bottom line? Taking action will make you mentally stronger in the long run. Who did you help along the way?

So, for all of you who have taken the time to invest in your career, can I count on you to reach back and pay it forward?

Is there a possibility to look at your situation with a different lens? If so, who can help you see things differently? This would be a great time to connect with your accountability partner or career coach. This is someone who has your best interest and would provide you with an honest look at yourself. Who can challenge the way you see things now? Commit to at least one action step to move your career forward.

I once again had to include the Mustiful effect on this career development journey. You know the line. It is the beautiful, wonderful, Mustiful action-oriented effect. It starts with me and ends with me. This is the one mantra I use to get myself moving whenever I get stuck. What is your effect? You can have that same positive effect. Be your own inspiration magnet. Let's get moving. Do not be discouraged. You get out what you put in.

Be honest with yourself; identify what it is that you know for sure about your potential. Are you ready to receive the feedback from the leadership assessment results? Do you have a trusted partner who will provide you with the truth about your potential? Once you have identified your potential, it is time to move forward. I am a big proponent of action. What is it that moves you to action? The self-saboteurs may enter your mind. Saboteurs are those thoughts that make you think that you cannot move to the next level or take on additional responsibility. So, if you are feeling scared or unsure about your dreams and you are thinking, "Am I really good enough?"

Write down your answers to the following questions:

- What is the worst that could happen if you reach your goals?
- What is the best that can happen if you reach your goals?
- What are you most excited about or what concerns come up for you as you think about your goals?
- Is it worth it to go all-in?

Surround yourself with people and thoughts that inspire success. Embrace the space of positivity. Be intentional about what you allow in your space. I get it. You cannot always escape the energy vampires that lurk in your workplace. Find the positive energy you need to move your career forward.

What do you want to be known for? Even if you don't think you are designing your legacy, that is exactly what you are doing. You are leaving an impression on people, whether it's positive or negative. Why not choose to lead by example and make your absence felt?

What keeps rising to the surface for you? Once you connect with your inner self, you will begin to see what is possible. Do not limit yourself to what you have always done. Bet on yourself. You will quickly begin to see even more possibilities.

"Time" and "action" were words that were rooted in my upbringing. When I reflect on my desire to be on time and take action, I am reminded how my thinking was shaped at an early age. I grew up with two planning messages from my parents: "Do it right the first time" and "Procrastination on your part does not constitute an emergency on mine." Subsequently, I sought out career opportunities that echoed those same sentiments. My career expectations for myself centered around time. Over the years, I played tug of war with time. Early in my career, the corporate culture that I experienced was centered on time and relationships. For example, if you arrived at a meeting on time, you were late. I do believe we should respect each other's time and, when we arrive early, utilize that time to learn more about our colleagues. If someone is consistently running late, why not hold them accountable for getting the information they missed? I would be interested to hear from you if the person who was running late was your colleague, what would you do? How would you handle that situation?

On the other hand, I have found that you can miss out on key life experiences if you don't yield to some type of flexibility. Those of us on the Judging dichotomy of the MBTI (Myers-Briggs Type Indicator) tend to value time as a high commodity. So many life lessons I have learned throughout my career. My focus on time was tested just trying to remember the days of the week during the pandemic. The one life lesson regarding time came from a good friend of mine who told me it was no longer necessary for me to remember the days of the week. Just focus your time on remembering yesterday, today, and tomorrow. Every day we are always making choices. Where you spend your time is a big choice. At the click of a button, you can be anywhere or do anything and you chose to take the time to read my book, *Navigating Your Next Career Move*, and I am grateful.

A NOTE TO LEADERS

How do you foster a courageous culture? Decide how you will nourish the talent of your team. Create an environment that nourishes them and gives them a sense of pride. Ask questions that focus on why they come to work every day. What do they want to achieve in the next six months? What could they be doing less of? When high performers work for great leaders, they let you know their passions. The mistake leaders often make is ignoring those conversations. As a manager, you can be so focused on getting to the next meeting that you are not listening to the meeting right in front of you. Ask yourself, are you the kind of leader others want to follow? True success is not just what you accomplish in your life or the lessons you help your team learn. It is about what you inspire others to do.

A grateful heart has served me well in my career.

CHAPTER SIX

DESTINATION GRATITUDE

Without courage, a person knocked off course will stay off course. Fear of making the wrong career move, not securing the big contract, or refining your skill set for the future will paralyze you from taking action. The comeback process requires that you gather a great deal of courage. When faced with career challenges and the uncertainty of the future, it will be important to ask for help, solicit career feedback, adopt self-care strategies, and practice daily gratitude.

One of the most effective ways to cultivate positive emotion is to practice gratitude. I'm sure you know the importance of keeping a gratitude journal. So, I encourage you to take it one step further and expand your thinking on gratitude. When you start writing in your journal or notebook, don't just name what you're grateful for, but also reflect on why you're grateful.

Research shows that when we reflect on why we're grateful and really think about what it means to us, it deepens our gratitude, and we experience even more positive emotions.

What are you carrying that keeps your mind on gratitude? When life gets you rattled, what is your response? Let's choose love, joy, peace, and calm. Life provides the cup; you get to choose what you fill it up with. So, I invite you to stop and ponder what you're grateful for, then reflect on why. What does it mean to you?

Maybe you're grateful for the ability to work from home, a

recent promotion, or a spouse or significant other that you didn't think you'd ever find. Maybe you're grateful for your kids and how healthy they are right now. Perhaps you or someone you love has recovered from COVID-19 or some other health challenge, and you're grateful because of a second chance at good health and life. Whatever it is that you're grateful for, taking time to reflect on the "why" behind your gratitude expands the positive emotion that you experience. In turn, the increase of positive emotion strengthens and equips you to better handle challenges, setbacks, and stress. It also helps you make better decisions, gives you a fresh perspective, and opens up your mind.

There is so much goodness that comes from positive emotions, and we must be intentional about building them. So, take some time today. Don't just think about what you're grateful for, also remember why you are grateful.

When you change what you say, you can change how you feel. Think through your daily to-do list for the week and think about the things you've said you have to do to take your career to the next level. We often talk about our to-do list and other responsibilities in terms of what we "have" to do, and yet speaking this way can create a sense of obligation.

Our thoughts often sound something like this: I have to go to work. I have to get this project done. I have to take my kids to school.

Next time, when you are thinking about your to-do list, try changing one word in your vocabulary from "I have to" to "I get to" and see how quickly your attitude changes. I get to work from home. I get to work on this project. I get to take my kids to school. The change in your words will enable two mental shifts: gratitude and expectation. Gratitude, of course, is what we are thankful for. Expectation is having something to look forward to. A simple shift in your words will remind you of everything you've been fortunate to have in your life. Choosing to speak from a place of gratitude about your responsibilities is the easiest way to fight the temptation to take the most important things in your life for granted.

It's very simple. When you find yourself saying "I have to," change the words to "I get to," and let it be a reminder of everything you get to be thankful for.

As you reflect on your career, what do you enjoy least about your role? What do you dread on your to-do list because you "have" to do it? For each thing you list in answer to the above question, ask, "Why am I grateful that I 'get to' do this?" What are the results you want to achieve?

What are you most grateful for right now and why are you so grateful for it?

How could you intentionally incorporate gratitude into your daily life?

Self-saboteurs are thoughts that enter your mind with the solo goal to create self-doubt. Some of those inner thoughts may read like this: "What are all the ways in which the idea won't work? How was I able to land this job? I am not ready to lead this initiative because I have not been in my role long enough." Stop the replay! These negative thoughts are centered on the fear of the unknown. Do not let yourself or anyone else drain your energy source.

The difference between those who bounce back and those who remain steadfast in their thinking is determined by how well they are able to manage the self-sabotaging thoughts that come to mind in the face of setbacks. Remember, resilient people act and think differently. They believe they can bounce back, and that belief leads to positive, intentional action steps.

Consider for a moment the fact that you have been in your current role for many years. Now you may be starting to feel stuck, or your mind continues to replay that you are not good enough to apply for a new position or take on a new role. Take a breath and choose YOU today. Choose to further develop your resiliency muscle.

Starting with an abundance mindset, let go of circumstances that are outside of your control. Focus on how the abundance mindset can help you take big risks for big payoffs. Work to foster connection with those around you. Now think about what a possible next step could be. Make a move. Learning sources are available. Have you tapped into all the resources available to you?

- Reach out to a friend from your #TeamLevelUp squad.
- Review the skills and experiences needed for a role you are interested in.
- Apply, apply, apply, and if you get the job, great; if you don't, that is great too. If it's an internal position, reach out to the hiring/recruiting manager and seek feedback on how you can prepare for the next interview. Other options you might consider helping you land your next position:
    1. Contact your HR department.
    2. Hire a career coach.
    3. Contact your mentor/Find a mentor.

Take into consideration the feedback you have received, step back, and then decide where you "get to" create change, improve, and grow. Receiving feedback is an opportunity to expand our thinking and pivot toward an actionable goal. The challenge we face in that moment can include conflicting messages, emotional responses, a visit from impostor syndrome, and the whispered voices of failures that have happened in our past. In that moment, how do we find our strength, revive our courage, and make the powerful pivot to our response of choice?

After reviewing the feedback, decide how best to move forward. The reality is you may not be able to act on all the feedback you have received. However, commit to taking at least one step toward making a change happen that will enhance your career development. It is important to create actionable change, drive accountability, and celebrate the positive potential of change, even in challenging times.

Continue to have a positive focus on your strengths to move

forward. Practice mindfulness as an active habit of gratitude. This is also a demonstration of resilience.

Accountability is an intentional practice. You are enough and are capable of making positive change. Let's take what you've learned, look at where you want to go, and craft a path that celebrates your talent and determination.

Ambition is your opportunity to refuse to quit on yourself. Did you notice there is a shift in the atmosphere? The shift in seasons when the days are longer and the nights are shorter. This may be your season of change. Change is all around us. At times it may feel uncomfortable. Other times it feels just right. Nevertheless, the seasons are changing. I look forward to the change of seasons. When I take time to enjoy the change of seasons, my gratitude meter shoots up exponentially. Think about it, when you read more, learn more, and are grateful, that type of mindset is always in season.

The world is constantly changing. How are you showing up in the midst of change? Take it one day at a time. Stay focused on the positive. What is this time of change teaching you about yourself? Positively, unequivocally, you are enough!

Today is another day to remain positive and be thankful. As you contemplate your definition of joy, think, *What do I need right now?*

What will support look like for you? If you think of your career as a continuous lifestyle, it may be easier to pinpoint the support needed to be successful. Start with guidance from your manager. What are the skills you should and could be developing as you grow in your career? Then shift to learning. What are the learnings you can develop on your own and with your colleagues? Is there an opportunity for a cube move, job shadowing, or cross-functional training? Next, garner insights on what specific skills you need to progress forward. Finally, identify those opportunities that will advance your career through jobs or projects that align with your interests.

You do not have control over how your day will turn out. The weather forecast may call for sunny with a 100 percent chance of letdowns. Nonetheless, you do have the opportunity to choose how you show up. How often do you capture those grateful moments in your life? Making time for what we are grateful for can simply start with a journal entry that says, "Another day to be thankful." I choose gratitude. I choose joy.

Joy can show up in the simplest of ways. When you come to the realization that the project's deadline must be adjusted because the team is not ready to launch the initiative, how do you turn that setback into joy? Sometimes the delay is necessary for the team to focus on the end goal and revisit the priorities.

Too often we hold our happiness hostage to our circumstances, insisting we will be happy when things change and get the position or contract we've been waiting for. What if you decided to be happy while you wait for things to come together? The truth is, if you are not satisfied no matter your circumstances, you'll likely find something to be unhappy about, even when your circumstances improve. Happiness is a choice, and sometimes not an easy one. You don't have to be happy about everything that happens in life, but you can choose happiness as a way of life despite what happens. Savor the challenging moments in your career as an opportunity to grow and count them as an opportunity for joy.

I have learned I cannot get everything done in a day. Do your best to focus on the most important things that can yield the highest impact. The prescription of gratitude has changed my life and if you start your day with joy, it will bring you more peace and less anxiety too. I want to reassure you that in times like these, it is normal to feel anxiety. Our stressors create thoughts, and those thoughts form our reactions. So, if your reaction to what you've seen and heard about the world around you has produced thoughts of anxiety, fear may be the natural response, meaning it's important to pay attention to what you're saying to yourself about what's been going on. And again, while it is normal to feel fear, we are not to operate out of that fear.

So how do we manage our fears and mitigate the spread of them? Take a moment to consider the following:

1. You have an internal compass, meaning there are some things you can control in order to take care of yourself or your loved ones. Take a moment to reflect, tune out the noise, and tune into yourself. Do not let fear win. The journey back to you is the priority. Ask yourself: What steps can I take to prioritize my health, the health of my family, and others who I care about?
2. There are external forces. These are things that are beyond your control. If your only focus is on the external, you can feel hopeless and helpless. What you must focus on is what is within your control. Ask yourself: What have I been anxious about that I cannot control?
3. Most importantly, it is important that when you can't control the outcome, you must trust the process. Ask yourself: What worries do I need to let go of in order to take one step forward?

When things are unsteady or don't seem normal, we cannot behave as though they are, which means it is important to take the time to reset our expectations of ourselves and the work environment.

If we don't reset our expectations, it can lead us to put pressure on ourselves to continue to go about our day as if everything is okay. As a result, we can end up feeling stressed, disappointed, or upset with ourselves and our present circumstances.

Consider these forward-thinking steps to help you reset expectations, be grateful, and be ready to pivot in the midst of career challenges:

1. What is working in your career, and what isn't working?

Start by taking a breath and a personal career inventory of what is preventing you from accomplishing what is most important right now. Trying to continue with "business as usual" could leave you feeling disappointed, discouraged, or unable to accomplish the goals you have set for yourself.

2. Experiment with your "new normal" to create a new routine.

It may take some time to figure out a new routine. It's okay to take the time to find out what works best for you! Personally, it has been helpful for me to set my intention for the day. What do I hope to accomplish today to bring me closer to my goal? Give yourself permission to do things differently than normal and take the time to focus on what you need and leave space for the unplanned in your day.

3. Practice self-care.

Most of you reading this have experienced a considerable number of changes in workload and responsibilities. Some of you have been working from home for over two years; some of you currently find yourselves working both as full-time employees and newly appointed teachers for your children; some of you are on the front lines of a pandemic, working every day, and some of you are working less or are without work entirely.

Some of the ways you can begin to incorporate self-care into your daily or weekly schedule include:

- Rest: We all understand that we need rest. Sleep clears out the stressors from the previous day. It's like hitting the reset button. Not only is it important to get enough sleep, but it's also important to have some moments throughout your day or week where you're not doing anything at all. This could be as simple as going to bed thirty minutes earlier or taking a few moments to be aware of your breaths (refer to chapter 4) throughout your day.

- Connection: Be present in your relationships, and actively listen and engage with the people in your life. Connecting in real ways with honest conversation fuels us. Who do you need to connect with? Who have you not been connecting with that energizes you? Even if you can't see them in person, a phone call or a Teams, FaceTime, or Zoom chat can be a great alternative way to connect. When we're able to be grateful through intentional connection, we get the energy to keep us going.

- Time release: Taking a time release is when you take the time to find something that truly engages every part of your mind and body. At the same time, it gives you a break from focusing on all the things you have to do or projects that you get to work on. We've all heard the phrase "work hard, play hard." Let's rewind back to the J dichotomy of the MBTI I mentioned earlier. This is an effective mindset shift. Doing something that's engaging but isn't "work" activates a different part of your brain, allowing the other side of your brain to rest. Letting one part of your brain rest, while actively engaging another part allows you to take a break from work. The stressors require a great deal of energy, and the release of those stressors allows you to come back to your work truly energized. A great self-care plan involves all three components. I challenge you to take some time and look at your schedule for the week and find ways you can incorporate each element into your week!

A NOTE TO LEADERS

To be able to take care of others, we have to take care of ourselves, and to do that we have to be intentional about rest and self-care. Notice where you are on the self-care spectrum, so you can help support your team and give them the opportunity to communicate where they are on the self-care spectrum. These seasons of change are so different from anything we have experienced. Rest, drink plenty of water, get outside, and go for a walk. Remember, exercise does not have to be intense or rigorous. It is getting up and taking that first step and expressing gratitude toward your team.

Collaborative Culture:
The Great Disruptor or The Great Reconnection?

CHAPTER SEVEN

COLLABORATIVE CULTURE

The year 2021 turned out to be the year of the Great Disruption. The disruption caused us to shift from the way we always did something to reimagining the possibilities of something new. This shift had us stepping back to reexamine what were the necessary behaviors, tools, and leadership actions to create real, long-term change.

In 2022, the Great Reconnection, we continued the need for emotional connectedness, while we stayed socially distanced. It's anyone's guess what the future will bring. Many companies have dedicated a lot of resources toward improving feedback mechanisms at every level of the organization. While I think that the initial focus of those resources has been to replace the traditional performance review model, that doesn't mean it can't be used for establishing a collaborative culture.

Why not work to rebuild your culture in a digital, hybrid world? Creating a forward-thinking culture starts with leveraging the feedback to empower the team. We have become a society that appreciates recommendations and feedback. As consumers, we get feedback via reviews on Amazon and status updates from our Instagram friends. On the work side, we rely on others to tell us about the candidate interview and their employee experience. And we use that information to make decisions about whether to apply or take the job offer.

Building a collaborative culture is what builds a collaborative organization. Improving employee engagement reduces turnover and improves overall work performance and helps to create a high-performing culture. The workplace has seen its share of discomfort, change, and even chaos. Human resources (HR) departments have been the catalyst in adapting to the constantly changing business landscape. HR continues to be the repository for all feedback from employees and their managers. HR professionals have seen massive changes in the way colleagues work, live, and play, and have had to adapt their advice accordingly. HR professionals must also be able to help their business unit leaders navigate the disruptive workplace trends while driving toward a high-performing collaborative culture. The change management process is intended to create environments where employees are encouraged to keep learning and make a leadership impact. The future of work is truly about inclusion. Leadership acumen is measured by a person's ability to transform diverse groups of people into cohesive, effective, and compassionate teams.

There are at least three ways to shift your mindset when you are in a state of influx and want to build or rebuild a collaborative culture. That includes evolving, inspiring, and thriving.

My hope is that your career has evolved as a result of reading my first book, *Aim High, Ask Why*. The intention of writing the book was to include real-life career and coaching experiences so you could decide how best to apply those learnings.

The world in front of us is drastically different than the world behind us. In the workplace, some pockets of the workspaces have evolved. There are elements of the way in which work has been exposed, and it is up to us to find our way back to inclusive learning. It is crucial that leaders get clear about what they need to do to evolve in an ever-changing culture to engage their employees, attract and retain talent, and build high-performing teams.

Expectations of people leaders continue to shift against the complex life, work, and social landscape we all continue to navigate. The goal is to take the time to guide people leaders to engage effectively and lead more inclusively so evolving leadership expectations are met.

Learning that includes diverse perspectives begins with a conversation. Conversation failures tend to happen when business results are high, key deliverables are missed, and team members start blaming and pointing fingers. As a result, situations go unresolved or are made worse.

Teams continue to evolve, realizing their biggest learnings come from a prior year full of change and priority shifts and the need to stop avoiding difficult conversations.

What happens when you need to have a difficult conversation so that you can foster alignment and agreement within your company culture? Where do you start? First, let's explore what is holding you back from having the conversation you need to have. Is it that you don't want to hurt that person's feelings? Could it be that your team member is going through a tough time, and you don't want to pile on additional work concerns? Whatever your reason, make it a point to have the conversation, today. If not today, tomorrow. Not next week or the week after that. Delaying the conversation does not make the situation go away or help to strengthen a collaborative culture. I often coach my clients on how to have the conversation at the snowflake level, not the snowball or avalanche level.

Often at the snowflake level, the snowflake appears and then disappears quickly. This is the level when you want to clear up any misconceptions or misunderstandings. Determine the main reason why you have not had the conversation. Seek first to understand each other's perspectives. When was the last time you listened to understand rather than to reply? Listening gives the other person the opportunity to let their voice be heard.

Don't let it get to the snowball level. The snowball level is where you have waited, procrastinated, and eliminated the opportunity to resolve the situation quickly. Listening with empathy is one of the most underrated communication and leadership skills. Listening with the intent to understand reduces misunderstandings and strengthens the connection between people and can lead to a collaborative culture.

Lastly, don't wait until the conversation reaches the avalanche level. At the avalanche level, emotions are high, and everyone involved thinks they are right and wants to take action immediately. It is important to recognize your role in the communication breakdown. When that person shares their version of the conversation, notice when you're thinking about your agenda versus theirs. Consider reflecting back on what you heard and setting up some norms for future interactions.

We are all reluctant to engage in behaviors that could negatively influence how others perceive our competence, awareness, and positivity. How do you create a brave space so that you are listening with intentionality? One way is to create psychological safety. Psychological safety is a belief that no one will be punished or humiliated for speaking up with ideas, questions, concerns, or mistakes. It's a shared belief held by members of a team that the team is safe to engage in interpersonal risk-taking.

From pandemic stress, workplace flexibility, and embracing hybrid work to psychological safety, we've had some highly impactful conversations over the past two years.

How does psychological safety play out in the workplace? Amy Edmondson is a professor of leadership and management from Harvard who studies people and teams seeking to make a difference through the work they do. A key takeaway from her research is that when you ask a question and listen to the response, you are saying, "I am interested in creating psychological safety."[7]

As you work to build or strengthen a collaborative culture, ask your team members questions like: What have you seen this week that could have been better? Think about your experience last

---

[7] *Building a psychologically safe workplace Amy Edmondson tedxhgse - youtube.* (n.d.). Retrieved June 16, 2022, from https://www.youtube.com/watch?v=BxC1Bl-4ZvE.

week, with your colleagues. Was everything as safe as you would like it to be? Let's consider the other extreme of the workplace culture. What if your project gets delayed? It could throw your timeline off track; your first instinct may be to get upset. It's okay to be disappointed. It's not productive to get upset and allow that to be a barrier to moving the project forward. A more productive response would be: now that the date has changed, what adjustments need to be made to the timeline? What do we need to do to get it back on track?

Inspiration. My company, Essence of Coaching, inspires leaders to rise to their potential. Inspiration is a forward-thinking word. For me, it invokes action. As we shift seasons, what have we learned about what inspires us? A great leader inspires you to have confidence in what you can do.

What do you need to do to level up on your leadership skills? For those of you who like to journal, write down your ideas on what would be your ideal future.

What if money and resources were unlimited? What dream would you pursue? Create a short-term goals list. Life can throw your goals into a tailspin. Revisit what goals are still attainable. Take the remaining steps to understand what realistic actions you will take to reach your goals by the timeline.

Where do you start? How do you create an interactive networking experience that allows you to explore the steps needed to be an inspiring and experienced leader? First, consider the ways you can focus on the most important areas for learning. Second, seek clarity on how you can positively impact these areas: leadership challenges, strategy development, funding and infrastructure, digitization, and creating your own personalized career development plan.

The levers that unleash leaders' greatest contributions are ensuring strategic clarity of purpose, accountability founded in integrity, and cross-functional relationships that inspire collaboration and trust.

The support for sustaining a collaborative culture comes from senior leadership. In our increasingly uncertain and complex business environment, companies must ensure their executives are not only advancing the bottom line but also working effectively across silos and inspiring teams to perform at their highest potential. Senior leaders, given their positional authority, receive much less feedback on their blind spots and effectiveness than they give to those that report to them. For those senior executives that do invite feedback from their colleagues, they may accept input about opportunities for improvement. They may resist the opportunity to connect the feedback to a clear, decisive plan of action that ensures changing their habits and behaviors while ensuring continuous business effectiveness.

Think about what else inspires you. Declutter something you have been avoiding for months. Let's start with your emails. With the number of emails we all get in a day, wouldn't it be great to organize your emails so they are easily accessible? The emails you no longer need, recycle them. Next, consider updating your contact list. Whether you have a Rolodex or a drawer full of business cards, determine which file system best serves you right now. As you determine those relationships you need to strengthen, what a perfect time to update your networking list.

Typically, when an idea is put into words, people can clearly understand the idea and it inspires action. When we focus on long-term success, we must also be willing to make short-term adjustments to get there.

To keep teams motivated amid industry and global changes, and drive toward a collaborative culture, leaders must keep three best practices top of mind.

1. Be versatile.

As an employee's work environment dramatically changes, the ability to look to an effective leader remains a constant that pays dividends when it comes to productivity.

"The hardest part of being a manager is coping with constant change; by the time your team masters a new process or work-flow, in an instant, the processes that you worked hard to build are suddenly disrupted," says Steve Fredette, president and co-founder of restaurant management platform Toast.

One way leaders are navigating these uncharted waters is by leveraging collaborative tools more frequently than they would if they were able to meet in person.

"It's important to over-communicate in times of change and chaos what the company is doing to respond in addition to help-ing your team get a broad outside perspective, especially the per-spective of your customers," says Fredette.[8]

2. Find opportunity in uncertainty.

While COVID-19 has wreaked havoc on individuals, families, and businesses, it has also forced executives to look inward when it comes to their leadership styles and spurred innovation across sectors.

"COVID-19 has served as a catalyst for a lot of organizations to reassess how they operate and how they motivate their teams to try new things and meet new challenges, which will ultimately mean positive, long-term changes," says David Henshall, CEO of remote work company Citrix. "My hope is that in the future, we don't need a deadly pandemic to force companies to be forward-looking about what is possible and embrace the chaos that comes with breakthrough innovation."[9]

This is felt by companies operating across industries. Anant Agarwal, CEO of online learning platform edX, has had to grap-ple with a surge in demand for online learning spurred by the spread of COVID-19, while also adapting his own workforce to

---

[8] Schwantes, M. (2020, August 31). *3 leadership practices that will help you get comfortable with Chaos.* Inc.com. Retrieved June 15, 2022, from https://www.inc.com/marcel-schwantes/3-leadership-practices-that-will-help-you-get-comfortable-with-chaos.html.
[9] Ibid.

remote environments. "In times of upheaval and chaos," he says, "it can be hard to move past the fear and anxiety chaos can induce. I found that motivating the team with the fact that our work truly mattered for learners during this period resonated the most."[10]

3. Where applicable, make it personal.

Traditionally, a C-suite's role in an organization has meant distance from day-to-day operations and the broad workforce. If you are in the C-suite, or planning to land there someday, you know the role often requires travel, so many leaders didn't have direct access to their employees, even if that's what they wanted.

While that access has changed the format of how we work, a global study of over 2,700 workers by Qualtrics and SAP during March and April 2020 found that nearly 40 percent said their company had not even asked them how they were doing since the pandemic began. More important, over 40 percent of people said they want their manager to introduce the subject.

Be intentional about checking in on your team. For example, once a month or more, ask non-business questions such as, what is your favorite vacation destination? What inspires you? What is your favorite sport or hobby outside of work?

Taking the time to check in with employees and ask how the pandemic is affecting them personally will not only allow leaders greater access to their workforce but will also open doors for future collaboration.

As you navigate through your career, it is important to keep in mind how you are showing up. What are qualities you want to embody as you position yourself for your next career move? Review the next few qualities and decide which ones resonate the most with you.

Curiosity.

Curiosity continues to be a driving force behind creativity and

---

[10] Ibid.

innovation, two highly desirable ways of looking at the world that are often in short supply in the (frequently) traditional world of business. Also, of value in an environment where companies are constantly on the lookout to improve processes with more agility and efficiency. Curiosity is a mindset that focuses on what can be done, not what can't.

Positive attitude.

The right tone goes a long way when you are looking to move up in your career. It makes a person easy to work with, which on a day-in-day-out basis is a significant asset. It also aligns with other areas like collaboration and team dynamics, always important from a management standpoint. Career success is how well you navigate the blueprint of your career path.

Resilience.

In business, as in life, things won't always go your way. You likely won't get every position you desire or every promotion or every bonus. At some point in your career, you will be faced with career disappointments. Therefore, your resilience, the ability to bounce back quickly from difficulties, is a key leadership trait. From a management standpoint, a resilient employee is a valued asset who can be counted on, most importantly, even when times are hard.

Willingness to learn.

Having an open mind and being willing to absorb new data and learn new skills are critical to employee success over the long term. Given the pace of change in today's business world, the ability and agility to adapt quickly matters; mental and psychological flexibility are key. The days when employees can simply succeed in a role by mastering a single set of tasks and repeating them over and over are no longer.

The best leaders are always striving to make sure the team thrives. Thriving means you are intentional about how you show up for your team. It is modeling the behavior you want to see in the team. Organizations that continue to thrive year after year are the ones that have cultivated extraordinary leaders. Extraordinary leaders are able to communicate strategy and help people see how they are connected to that strategy. Extraordinary leaders support collaboration and innovation. Leaders are passionate about the work they do. They see their role as a conduit to ensure individuals and teams rise to their potential. Leaders who thrive, work harder to share feedback, and show appreciation, become more efficient in their roles and that yields sustainable business and team results.

Feedback.

We should always embrace feedback. Seek it out and view it as a gift. If we think about feedback as a gift, we can then thank the giver. As the receiver of the feedback, you get to decide how you will act on it. What specific area of the feedback do you want to work on? Leaders share with their team members what they do well and what they need to do even better. The timing and location of the feedback are important things to consider when delivering feedback.

Show appreciation.

Appreciation comes in many forms and does not always have to cost a lot of money. Have you read books on ways to show appreciation? There must be at least 2,022 ways to show appreciation. When was the last time you said "thank you" to someone? The little things make the biggest difference.

- Take time to write someone a thank you note.
- Encourage people to achieve their career aspirations.

- Listen to new innovative ideas.
- Laugh often, especially at yourself.
- Rely on email/voicemail less and talk to people more.

These past two years have shown, after months of working remotely, that leaders are tired, burned out, and barely have the bandwidth to take care of themselves, let alone support their team. As return-to-work dates continue to get pushed further away, it is time to stop waiting for the storm to pass and learn to thrive in our new reality. Leaders need to continue to learn ways to engage in a remote, collaborative culture.

Cultivating resilience professionally requires a clear understanding of how we personally navigate adversity. As leaders, when change and challenges arise, it is important to focus on your priorities while establishing a purpose-driven approach to inspire and equip everyone on the team to thrive. Resilience isn't just about bouncing back from adversity, but rather, having a resilient mindset enables us to capture lessons learned and challenge our thinking as we move forward in a more effective and efficient way.

Strategically driving organizational effectiveness through change and uncertainty during a normal business period isn't easy—you know that. The impacts of the COVID-19 pandemic significantly changed how we now do business. Why not take advantage of and initiate change that strategically and decisively positions you and your workforce for even greater flexibility, agility, and success? Why not take this time to step up and show your organization how to drive, survive, and thrive in change and uncertainty?

Leaders, take the initiative, be innovative, and seek insights from your team on ways to be more productive. The team needs the right environment to thrive. You can create that thriving environment by not only recruiting employees on your team but also making sure you are attracting and retaining talent. Guess what? When we collaborate, we all shine brighter.

The simple things in life usually turn out to have a lasting positive impact. Your team members have a unique ability to connect with people, bring calm to unpleasant situations, and look at things from a strategic point of view. Embrace that!

I state this in my first book, *Aim High, Ask Why*, and I will state again: development is all about YOU! You are the ultimate driver that gets to design your career path forward. You get to take your career to the next level! You get to choose how you want to show up for work every day. Take the good with the bad. Take the bitter with the sweet. Spread your wings and explore what will be your new normal.

How can you gain support from your manager? One way is to manage up. Try to anticipate the needs of your manager. This approach demonstrates your ability to influence and deliver results. Remember, whether you are a manager or aspire to be a manager, model the behavior you want to see in others.

While we may turn off the chaos when we leave work at the end of the day, we do know that no two days are the same. Your career path will continue to be filled with ups and downs, twists and turns. The more you practice ways to overcome life's curve, the better you can become at getting ahead of the fast pitches or career barriers.

Strengthening a collaborative culture can begin with you and how you navigate your career. Have you considered rebooting your professional development routine? This could be the perfect time to change how you go about your development. With each new season, there come changes. How are those business changes showing up in your workplace? What are the latest competencies or skill sets that will be needed in the next fiscal year? Think of your career development as a muscle. In order to get stronger, you have to use it. Let it become a part of your lifestyle and it will not seem like work.

The best investment you can make is in yourself. You have the knowledge within you to move your career forward. The best way to find out if your idea will work is to try it. It doesn't matter when you start. It doesn't matter where you start. All that matters is that you start. Make the most of your time. Is it possible to outwork yesterday? You have the wherewithal to direct your career path. What goal would stretch you beyond your comfort zone? Here are some tips that may help you stick to your goals.

- Find out what motivates you. The power of inspiration is a helpful tool to get you to the finish line.
- Accountability partner. Partner with someone who is moving in a positive direction and wants to see you succeed.
- Anticipate challenges. Be ready for obstacles. In your development, it may seem as though you are taking steps backward. Keep pushing forward.
- Reward. Recharge after each milestone. Give yourself a pat on the back or a high five. You put in the work. Now celebrate.

What assessment tools have you used lately? First, begin with understanding your strengths. As you build your career toolbox, seek opportunities that align with your strengths and do what you really love to do. Next, move toward refining your opportunities for development. We all have blind spots we need to work on. Identify at least one that you will commit to sharpening within the next six months. What are you passionate about? The answer to that question will lead you to your purpose. You are awesome. Today is yours. Make the most of it! In addition to performing at a high level, take these focus areas with you along the journey. Remember, career development is a lifestyle!

- Clarity: Get clear about your purpose. Define who you are, who you want to be, and use it for a purpose greater than yourself.
- Capability: Ask courageous questions. What can I do to rise to my potential? What am I willing to do to stretch outside of my comfort zone?
- Curiosity: Explore the possibilities. Ask why. Do

not shy away from the tough questions that give you insight into what you need to work on.

It is so important to know that you have options. Prepare yourself for the next position so that you don't become dependent on a job or another person, but you depend on yourself. You will eventually hit your morning stride. Trust the timing of your life. Stay determined, stay focused, and, most of all, trust your journey. Success is hard work, persistence, doubts, late nights, rejections, sacrifices, discipline, criticism, failures, and risks. I believe this is the inspirational recipe for success. Be inspired. Do not look back. You are not going that way. Look ahead, so you can see what inspires you to aim high, ask why, and live your best life. We have to hold on to our dreams.

A NOTE TO LEADERS

We all know what a toxic culture feels like, and we all know what it feels like to work in a collaborative culture. What's missing from the tool belt of many executive teams is how to establish a clearly defined positive code of behaviors, mindsets, and conduct. These need to be collectively understood and practiced every day in how people show up, impact each other, and approach their work. I invite you to consider how you can create a climate of openness where people feel free to talk about errors and share their failures and engage in creativity and innovation. You can create a space where the team redefines the great reconnection. You can also strengthen relationships by building workplace connections one at a time, including leadership support in the onboarding process, and encouraging team members to ask for help when needed.

Leaders should create opportunities for their team members to be recognized for their work. While diversity, equity, and inclusion may have been a part of strategic plans for years, there is an urgency in the execution of those plans to foster impactful and sustainable change. You can foster that change by focusing on employees' strengths. Focusing on strengths is a winning strategy for building an inclusive work culture. When leaders prioritize the understanding and cultivating of their team members' strengths, that conveys appreciation for what that team member brings to the table. Diversity is listening, learning, and leaning so the conversations and actions further rebuild a highly supportive workplace. Be intentional about shifting from transactional approaches to diversity, equity, and inclusion to transformational approaches that result in long-term sustainable impact. Diversity, equity, and inclusion can't be a short-term goal. They need to be incorporated into the company values.

If we can innovate ways to explore outer space, surely, we can dedicate resources to innovate collaboratively around diversity, equity, and inclusion. Representation matters, choose to help build a world where we are all included.

Leadership is a path forward to help those around us rise.

Chapter Eight

Rise Up!

Rise up and create a path forward! Invest in yourself. Stay curious. As you reflect on your career to date, what has the pandemic taught you about yourself? How do you make sure you do not bring forward what needs to be left behind? What are your strengths that stand out from all the others? What did you learn or unlearn from your manager?

Take time to reflect on accomplishments from your career. What have you learned about yourself throughout the pandemic? At some point, you probably created boundaries for yourself. Having an awareness of what you will and won't do is necessary. Get clarity on what type of work is fulfilling and what feels like a routine.

Have you ever had a conversation with your manager and after the meeting you were like, *WTF?* Your first thought to yourself may have been if only your manager would have taken the time to see you and hear you. As you read the following statements, think about if you have ever had a similar experience.

- You schedule a one-to-one meeting with your manager with the hopes of discussing your career path, the topic is in the subject line of the meeting invite, and quickly the conversation shifts to the status of the projects that are due by end of day instead of the support you need to develop your career path.

- In preparation for your one-on-one meeting with your manager, you arrive to the Zoom meeting early, prepared and organized, and at the conclusion of the meeting, there is no acknowledgment of the work you've done to move the project forward.
- You share with your manager your thoughts about your next career move, and you are met with a look of disbelief. Your manager's response: "Surely, you do not expect to move up in the organization, you have only been with the company for a year."
- After multiple discussions with your manager with no focus on your career path, you start to feel a shift. You have reached a fork in the road. So, what do you do now? Well, your options are to fight, take flight, or freeze. I shared a personal story in my first book, Aim High, Ask Why, of the approach I took to help me make the decision to take flight on my latest career path. I believe there is a strong correlation between leaders not leaving companies and choosing to leave managers. When you don't feel valued, seen, or heard, you begin to map out an exit strategy that includes where you will go to feel appreciated and valued.

A different option to consider is to seek other career opportunities within the organization. Do I build or buy? If I consider building/leveraging my talents in another department, that gives me the opportunity to build my leadership muscle and expand my leadership responsibilities. Sometimes, your manager may not support that option because it may make your manager look bad and that option is no longer a consideration. If I select the option to buy, that now places me into the now-famous alumnus group of 2021: the Great Resignation. The world of work is changing daily.

You have workers who are joining the Great Resignation space, employers who are expanding their remote workers' space, and the workforce is rethinking how they are looking for their next job.

THE GREAT RESIGNATION

I categorize this as a time in 2021 when people within organizations decided their worth or career experience was not being recognized. In the spring and summer of 2021, workers resigned from nearly twenty million jobs. The result: you make the decision to resign and take your talent elsewhere—not the infamous St. Elsewhere, but to a place where you will feel valued, seen, and heard.

The Great Resignation was seemingly the word of the year in 2021. Many leaders were puzzled about why people were leaving their jobs. The short answer was people were exhausted. The notion that leaders could not find good talent was unbelievable. If you can't find good talent in one place, then you go someplace else. Where are you searching for the talent? The way in which you recruited talent ten years ago will not bring you successful talent this year.

Working remotely started out as a perk for some, for others, it was a chaotic whirlwind. For several people, working from home did not just include the employee, it also included four-legged roommates, children who were not vaccinated, and parents who did not feel comfortable taking them to school. It also included caring for elderly parents who did not have access to the COVID-19 vaccine. So, again I say, remote working was not a perk for most. The thought of going back to a cubicle was a stress-inducing experience. One suggestion for leaders on how to move from the Great Resignation to the Great Reconnection is to compare the needs of the business to the needs of their most important commodity: your people. Amplify what you offer your employees, health insurance, 401(k) matches, sabbatical, and hybrid work schedules that allow employees to take a vacation and not come back to the same situation. I believe people want to do their best work. They also want to know their work is appreciated. When was the last time you asked a team member how they like to be recognized? Rewards and recognition continue to be the way in which leaders can show their teams how much they appreciate the work they do.

THE ESCAPE ROOM

This was designed to be a teambuilding activity for all involved to use their skills and wit to decode clues and unlock doors to ultimately escape the room by a certain time period and celebrate with a win. When I think about how I have navigated my career path over the years, there was a similar framework. Within the politics of corporate America, I chose to seek out mentors to help me navigate through the minutia and quickly move up the corporate ladder. One of my mentors reminded me frequently, as I was progressing along my career path, to make sure I laughed often, lived life to the fullest, knew when it was time to leave, and celebrated my wins. What growth did you experience in the prior year that you need to celebrate? Be proud of the steps you have taken to advance your career. Even if it may have taken you longer, you still achieved your goal. What do you want to do differently as you progress forward? The strategy you used in 2021 may not be the strategy that will be needed for the journey ahead. When you take time to reflect, learn, and dream about what's next, you invest in yourself as a leader.

LASTING INFLUENCE

In my book, *Aim High, Ask Why*, I share my thoughts on leaving a lasting influence and ultimately leaving a legacy. Take the time to leave breadcrumbs for those who will see your career path and create a path of their own. Show up as a leader who gives their team the tools and shortcuts to be successful in their roles.

How are you showing up in your workspace? Zoom space? Hybrid place? Are you a trendsetter? A trendsetter does their research. They are well aware of the skill set that is needed for the short term, and what skills are going to be needed in the future. Sometimes in your career, you can manage up and help your leader identify solutions to their pain points. Pain points help you seek clarity on what is getting in the way of proactively delivering on the needs of the client. Deciding how to deliver scalable solutions to accelerate the growth patterns of your internal and external customers is key. How do you position yourself to be the difference-maker? Start with your immediate network. Lean into ideas that can help you move strategic initiatives forward.

Purpose-driven—renew your own sense of purpose and meaning. What do you want to focus on in your career? What is your *why*? How will you know? Start by listing out what about your day-to-day work brings you joy and meaning. I reference in *Aim High, Ask Why*: think about what part of the work you do causes you to jump out of bed and hit the alarm clock the first time. For most of your career, you may have taken on roles that align with your trade, hobby, or collegiate degree. You may have taken on careers solely for the salary potential. You may have taken an interest in jobs because of the people and benefits the company offers.

Let's suppose in your go-forward season, you decide you want to have more joy, experience more growth opportunities, and align your next career move with your purpose. How would you describe the go-forward season? Are you surrounded by people who are cheering you on? Do you feel supported by your manager? Peers? Business partners? What are the initial steps you can take to make your purpose-driven season a reality? Who do you trust to take this journey with you? Note to self: everyone may not be as excited about your go-forward season. Everyone does not get the benefit of taking up the front-row seats on this journey. So, make sure you set boundaries and intentions on how best to navigate the best course for you and who is in your cheering section.

KEEP GOING!

The end of another day may seem daunting to you . . . keep going.

You may be at a fork in the road, and you need to decide whether to continue to work from home or go into the office . . . keep going!

One more project has landed in your inbox with a high-priority alert along with the other two projects, you received an hour ago . . . keep going!

The world view may not match your personal view . . . keep going!

A friend may have let you down . . . keep going!

You need to decide whether to home school, go to school, or Zoom school . . . keep going!

How do you keep going when you don't feel like moving? Start expecting wonderful things to happen. Recognize a setback as a setup for success. Be grateful and prepare to rise up.

How often do we focus on the big things and lose sight of the little things? We had grown so accustomed to having busy schedules and accumulating things. Sometimes that busyness causes unnecessary stress and anxiety. Would it be possible to start your week focusing on the small things, so the big things don't seem so big?

Here's a start: This week, stay focused on the numbers. Write down the number one reason you do what you love and love what you do. Share two new ideas on how you will expand your network. Name three things you are grateful for. List four things that inspire you to move forward. Write down five reasons your attitude lines up with your gratitude. You are on your way! Stay focused!

As a leader, you play a vital role in planning and directing the work assignments in your work teams. Continue to clarify the expectations for the position, the skills and knowledge your direct reports will need to be an effective leader, and offer a path to follow to successfully lead others.

You don't have to have "manager" in your job title to be a leader. You'll find people with leadership qualities throughout companies and organizations who encourage their colleagues, inspire others, bring forward innovative ideas, and perform well. Becoming a better leader can make you one of your company's strongest assets and put you on track for a senior leadership position.

A sense of self-awareness or understanding your own strengths and weaknesses can lead to higher emotional intelligence. Being a better communicator, especially a good listener, can make all the difference when you need to negotiate or resolve a conflict between team members. Whether working one-on-one with an employee or rallying your whole team, interpersonal skills will help you cultivate workplace success and success in others.

Understand your potential and develop vital skills to progress your leadership, personal growth, and career success.

While some level of technical expertise is necessary for management positions, depending on the specific position, it is also important that leaders:

- Model appropriate behavior. Character issues trickle down to employees, often resulting in a lack of discretionary effort, company loyalty, and inappropriate behavior.
- Are patient. Going slowly in the beginning earns the respect and credibility necessary to make changes. Making changes and quick decisions when first starting as a new manager or managerial role can hurt your effectiveness.
- Learn the skill sets of their direct reports. What are an employee's strengths and weaknesses? Knowing who is good at what is critical to getting work done.
- Are visible and accessible. The more accessible a manager is, the smaller the "learning curve" for getting to know and understand your team. The more a manager reaches out to the team for check-ins, the more dialogue will take place. Being visible also improves productivity, the mere presence of a manager communicates to the employee that you see them and appreciate the quality of their work.

As a first-time manager, you are responsible for getting the work done through your people. How you approach that responsibility is a reflection of your leadership style. Some managers tend to interact with the team solely just to get the job done. These managers are viewed as having a task-oriented leadership style. Other managers tend to put more emphasis on their relationships with people and less emphasis on getting the job done. These managers are viewed as having a people-oriented leadership style. Whether you tend to be more task-oriented or more people-oriented will affect the way you manage others.

In summary, the most effective senior leaders can think, act, and influence at both a tactical and strategic level, balancing strategic priorities to help the organization achieve its goals.

As you think about the competencies needed for your career path forward, it will be important to continue focusing on getting results amidst ambiguity, influencing change, and improving the effectiveness of your interpersonal behaviors.

Use this season of learning to gain awareness about your strengths and developmental needs as a leader.

- Demonstrate effective communication and collaboration skills across the organization.
- Learn how to balance strategic and operational goals to align with the company mission.
- Gain skills to influence others amidst change and ambiguity.

As you think about advancing your career, consider the importance of knowing how to be organizationally agile with strategy, people, processes, and systems across the organization. Also knowing how to strengthen and deepen relationships to bridge differences and build strategic ties helps to balance competing priorities.

Most importantly, start and end the day with a positive word, post it and keep repeating it. Mindset shifts are when we happily expand our thinking to include positive thoughts. If everyone had an open mindset, and a willingness to share successes, we could share more success stories and opportunities on how to rise up to the next level of leadership, one leader at a time.

A NOTE TO LEADERS

Leaders, create an inclusive culture that attracts and retains leaders with diverse perspectives and fosters design thinking. Appreciate the small wins. How can you bring out the best in yourself and the best in others? As a leader, make sure the teams' decisions are aligned with the organizational values, and are fact-based and inclusive. Take time to create intentional ecosystems so employees become more engaged, which yields a positive impact on productivity and profitability.

Strengthen your leadership muscle by making sure each person on your team knows they are valued and appreciated. You can influence the way your team collaborates by establishing heartfelt connections and encouraging meaningful conversations. Have you considered a four-day work week? Working fewer hours while focusing on efficiency will attract and retain talented team members and improve mental well-being, productivity, and team communication.

Encourage your team not to tie their worth to a title or position. You model the way by establishing boundaries that inspire every-one to do their best and not at the expense of their mental well-being or time on the job.

"Women of color are amazing.
Don't stand by and watch our talent be wasted, or worse,
contribute to the problems many of us face in corporate structures."
—Dr. Ella Bell, Tuck School of Business, Dartmouth College

CHAPTER NINE

FINAL THOUGHTS

Women in leadership. How do we address the female leadership gap? For starters, we can't act like it doesn't exist, because it does. As women in leadership, I encourage you to keep working on skills like communicating the company's strategic vision and managing risk. These are leadership skills of the future and essential to securing top leadership roles. Women leaders of the future will need to continue focusing directly on strengthening negotiation skills, navigating challenging group dynamics, and overcoming organizational roadblocks by employing effective leadership skills.

Women that are beginning their careers in business often aspire to top leadership positions, perhaps even CEO. Sometimes their career ladder includes entrenched gender bias in organizations and that ambition doesn't always translate into promotions. Women will create the future we need and not the one that has been offered to us.

I have personally been the only woman on the senior executive leadership team. I have also been the first and only executive woman of color in the C-suite. To that point, while in corporate America, I had a great experience. I learned a tremendous amount, and it really sensitized me to the challenges that other women leaders are faced with daily in organizations. Negative stereotypes about women as senior leaders of the organization continue to exist. Women are often met with the narrow goal of obtaining a seat at the corporate table. As if there is only one seat. We can make more room for more seats at the table. The success of women doesn't have to come at the cost of others.

What specifically can women do to overcome these roadblocks to move into those senior positions? Or, if we're already in those senior positions, how do other leaders help build a culture for other women? Read and take actionable steps by reading the "Woman of Color Reimagining the World of Work." It's a report put out by nFormation and the Billie Jean King Leadership Initiative that covers the topic from the problem through to solutions, breaking it down so the reader can fully understand, and empathize with, the WOC perspective.

More and more women continue to take control of their careers and make decisions based on what is best for them/family. If you want different, you must move different! Only you know how best to make your body move. There's nothing more powerful than a woman who is working to create the life she knows she deserves while remaining grateful for the one she has been given.

Be clear about the work that brings you joy. It is not about balance; it is about harmony. There will be seasons of stressful work and other seasons where you should slow down and be more present. Appreciate the time as you move through each season and reflect on the lessons the season is teaching you about yourself.

The most senior level of leaders will need to play an integral part in encouraging women to seek leadership roles. Women, surround yourself with women who would mention your name in a room full of opportunities.

"Know your worth—you must find the courage to leave the table if respect is no longer being served."
—Tene Edwards[11]

My hope is that existing leadership—male and female—will have broader, out-of-box, action-oriented conversations about how to advocate for more female leaders to successfully rise to their potential. For now, let's celebrate the continued notable achievements of women shattering glass ceilings from heads of state, CEOs of the world's largest corporations, legacy educational institutions, the arts, and self-made women billionaires.

What does next-level leadership look like? A leader reads the environment, then adapts and adjusts within it to achieve determined goals. Rather than create a direction of his/her own, a leader prides themself on the ability to implement the goals of others by astutely managing his/her environment. A leader plays the matrix game almost to perfection. A leader displays the considerable passion that a leader applies liberally. A leader thinks emotionally and often through associations, making judgments through loyalty, pride, and an uncompromising desire to succeed. A leader measures most issues in terms of how important the issues are to the bottom line. A leader intends to succeed, and in their pursuit of success, a leader drives themself so hard a leader has little time for reflection and perspective. While intensely ambitious, a leader also possesses a strong need to belong and succeeds by meeting the expectations of those the leader hopes will accept them into the fold.

Leaders who intend to succeed and in the pursuit of success can drive themselves so hard, there is little time for reflection and perspective. Leaders set the stage for personifying the need to be

---

[11] Quotespedia.org. (2020, July 11). *Know your worth. you must find the courage to leave the table if . . .* Quotespedia.org. Retrieved June 15, 2022, from https://www.quotespedia.org/authors/t/tene-edwards/know-your-worth-you-must-find-the-courage-to-leave-the-table-if-respect-is-no-longer-being-served-tene-edwards/.

compassionate, resilient, and adaptable. Leaders also need to create a brave environment for the team to feel heard, seen, and understood. Leaders tend to be highly conscientious and dedicated. Leaders do what needs to be done with unfailing loyalty. They accept tough goals, then inspire others to attain them. Leaders manage others quite loosely, expecting them to become inspired and determine their own course. Leaders tend to give quick feedback when progress is lacking, or mistakes are made. If a leader has direct reports, a leader expects that their directs will approach them with their visions and concerns. Rather than set the course, a leader finds ways to implement it.

While a leader is an expert at managing the organization toward common goals, he/she has yet to set their own expectations for performance. Their drive for perfection and their history of working for controlling and often dominating personalities prevent them from determining their own set of standards and pursuing them over time. A leader's style of constantly managing the changing day-to-day scene prevents them from looking into the future and clearly defining what they want to accomplish. While he/she reacts brilliantly and effectively in response to changing conditions and a superior's demands, he/she has yet to set specific goals of their own and pursue them with the diligence they expect of their directs. A leader must move beyond "it depends" directly toward "this is what I expect."

To become fully effective as a leader, make sure you set clear expectations for those in your area of responsibility. Rather than react to what they do, a leader needs to define what they want their team to do and monitor their progress over time. A leader sets their own expectations, sells those expectations to the organization then monitors compliance with those expectations over time. Growing as a leader requires you to embrace new challenges, overcome something that is difficult or do something you have never considered doing.

What do I know for sure? I am confident there is no going back to the way things were. I also believe professional development is a constant cycle of growth. The growth is happening inside and outside of the workplace. We do not have an endless supply of time, yet when we use the time that we do have, we can make a difference. Jobs are temporary and careers, when developed with intention and purpose, can last a lifetime. The greatest lesson from the COVID-19 pandemic is that your greatest wealth is your health.

Look at your career from the top shelf and do what you love and love what you do. I encourage you to ask more questions and get clarity on your purpose. I am holding space for you to see the best inside yourself and develop action steps to get there. Keep rising to your potential!

How do you become more confident with your own abilities and strengths? How do you create a more inclusive culture from where you sit?

Continue to address the systemic changes that are needed to rebuild the inequities that are underneath the surface.

- Understand the other person's point of view.
- Accept values and opinions that are different than your own but don't accept bad behavior.
- Identify your feelings before you share your concerns with another (remember to pause before you speak).
- Talk directly to people that have engaged in disrespectful behavior.
- Model kindness in your responses; do not blame, threaten, or name call, even when you are annoyed or hurt; apologize when appropriate.
- Practice respect and kindness.
- Be a part of the solution and not part of the problem.

Check-in with your manager and express your thoughts on how the company can ensure all employees contribute and are provided opportunities to create in a more collaborative way and discuss options on how to remain engaged. Leadership needs to challenge questionable behaviors with confidence in a timely and efficient manner.

Be motivated to make an impact. My hope for you is that your vision remains clear. May the odds be in your favor. Lead the way by making a difference every day and position yourself to develop the next generation to pass the baton. Don't forget, when you accomplish amazing things in your life, reach back and bring someone with you. It is a new day and great things are happening!

And just like that . . . I thank you for allowing me to join you as you *navigate your next career move*. Make sure your next move is your best move. Keep taking your career to the next level!

Acknowledgments

In honor of the greats on whose shoulders I stand, thank you; this one is for you. Because of you, I understood the assignment, clutched my pearls, wore the heels needed to shatter the glass ceilings, and took my career to the next level. I am forever grateful.

A special thanks to my leadership squad. You are true thought partners that jumped in and cheered for me beyond the finish line. You helped me bring this book into the world to be shared by all who are inspired to reach their highest potential.

I am ever so grateful to my amazing family who continues to create space for me to be my best self, extend me grace as I learn more, and remind me to enjoy every breath, one day at a time.

ABOUT THE AUTHOR

Sonja Mustiful is the principal and owner of Essence of Coaching, a leadership development consulting firm dedicated to inspiring business professionals to rise to their potential.

With over fifteen years of human resource management and executive coaching experience, Sonja has acquired the competencies needed for the next level of leadership and is also the author of *Aim High, Ask Why: Discover Strengths, Uncover Blind Spots, and Rise to Your Potential*.

Gleaning information from numerous leadership interviews, corporate business partnerships, and life experiences, rapid-selling author and leadership-development strategist Sonja Mustiful shares practical insights on how you can put these leadership development tools to work immediately. Her insightful approach has helped inspire leaders and clients to realize they are capable of far more than they know.

Instagram: @SonjaTheCoach

LinkedIn: Sonja Mustiful

To continue the learning, sign up to join the next Aim Higher Leadership Development Cohort Series.

Aim Higher™ Leadership Development Cohort Series

The Aim Higher™ Leadership Program is a four-week live online workshop series designed for participants who want to maximize their leadership impact. Through engaging dialogue, guided activities, and reflection assignments, you will have tools that showcase who you are as a leader and an opportunity for guided practice to rise to your potential. You will learn how to leverage your strengths to make a greater impact through courageous and transformational leadership.

- Increase your emotional intelligence and effectiveness.
- Uncover limiting narratives that deter leadership influence.
- Develop effective, interpersonal communication skills.
- Identify leadership Strengths, Blind Spots, Values, and Purpose.

www.essenceofcoaching.com

OTHER BOOKS
BY SONJA D. MUSTIFUL

Aim High, Ask Why: Discover Strengths Uncover Blind Spots, and Rise to your Potential

Aim Higher Leadership Development Series: Discussion Guide